Cover photograph: *Fig. 28* 2. Eakins, Susan Macdowell Eakins.
c. 1884. Collection of Walter Macdowell,
Roanoke, Va.

Thomas Eakins:

His Photographic Works

Pennsylvania Academy of the Fine Arts

Philadelphia, Pennsylvania 1969

Contents

Foreword

The role of Thomas Eakins as a photographer has historically been either understated or misunderstood, sometimes both. It remained for Mr. Gordon Hendricks, probably the most indefatigable researcher working in the American field today, to reveal the true dimensions of Eakins' photography. Unearthing family scenes, genre, portraiture, and landscapes, Mr. Hendricks lets us appreciate at once the independent beauty and art historical significance of the photographs.

The Academy is delighted to be able to present this critical survey of Eakins' photography and to simultaneously salve its nearly century-old pangs of conscience. We are, of course, extremely grateful to Mr. Gordon Hendricks for the privilege of working with him in this regard.

Moreover, we are gratified to be cooperating, in a small way, with the Eakins House Restoration Committee, itself ably co-chaired by Mr. Theodore Newbold and Mr. Daniel Dietrich, II, whose additional generosity as a lender is exemplary. The Metropolitan Museum of Art and the Philadelphia Museum of Art also have been most supportive, as has the Joseph H. Hirshhorn Collection. We also appreciate the generous loans of Mr. Walter Macdowell and Mr. Donald Stephens.

Appreciation (and sheer admiration) is also extended to Mr. Rolf Petersen and the other photographers, whose creative recreation of the vulnerable and fading Eakins prints has been a joy to behold.

Lastly, to my staff, particularly Mrs. Christine Jones Huber and Miss Susan Whitin, my sincere appreciation for their bouyant spirits and untiring efforts during their first exhibition. The Academy is pleased to be able to circulate this exhibition nationally and hopes it will significantly add to the appreciation of a great American artist.

William B. Stevens, Jr., *Director*
Pennsylvania Academy of the Fine Arts

Preface

An exhibition of the photographs of Thomas Eakins was first suggested to me by Jacob Deschin at a cocktail party given by Barbara Morgan in honor of Ansel Adams in April of this year, 1969. The previous year, after a lecture at Smith College, Leonard Baskin had asked me to write a book for his Gehenna Press on Eakins as a photographer. Soon I unearthed a great many unknown, beautiful and significant photographs by the artist.

Kneeland McNulty of the Philadelphia Museum of Art and Beaumont Newhall of the George Eastman House both encouraged me to proceed with the project and made helpful suggestions. Dan Dietrich, co-chairman of the Eakins house restoration committee, was a constant, helpful friend. The critical point came, however, when Dr. Edgar P. Richardson, President of the Pennsylvania Academy of the Fine Arts, suggested that I propose such an exhibition to the Academy's new Director, William B. Stevens, Jr. "The Academy owes something to Eakins' memory," Dr. Richardson said. Mr. Stevens' response was prompt and enthusiastic, and in the short period between August, when the exhibition was decided upon for the Academy, and January, when it was to open, our work together has been headlong and our association congenial and stimulating. Above all, Mr. Stevens was, like myself, "turned on" by Eakins' photographs.

I am particularly grateful to Miss Frances Crowell for her kind cooperation, and to her sister Dr. Caroline Crowell and her brothers Will Crowell and Dr. James Crowell. I am grateful to Donald Stephens and his wife Inga for many helpful, convivial conversations, also to Mrs. Rebecca Garrett, Mrs. Francis Walters, and Walter Macdowell. It has been an exhilarating experience to talk to these kind friends about their Uncle Tom.

I am also grateful to members of the staff of the Academy for intelligent, enthusiastic help: Christine Jones and Susan Whitin, in particular, and my long-time friend Louise Wallman, who had already been helping me with Eakins research for some years. Besides those already mentioned, good advice and encouragement was given me by Guido Castelli, Joseph Fraser, Frank Gettings, Cynthia Jaffe, Abram Lerner, A. Hyatt Mayor, and Emily Umberger. I also owe a debt to the talent and patience of Gene Feldman who designed and produced the catalogue.

Much credit should be given to Rolf P. Petersen for his kind advice, illuminating conversation, and the distinguished talent he brought to bear upon the preparation of negatives and reproduction and exhibition prints from many badly faded and marked original photographs. Mr. Petersen is responsible for the negatives and prints from my own collection, those of Mr. and Mrs. Daniel W. Dietrich, II, and Walter Macdowell. A.J. Wyatt has prepared the Philadelphia Museum's negatives and prints, William Pons those of the Metropolitan, and O.E. Nelson those of the Hirshhorn collection.

One important question remains: how do we know the photographs in the exhibition are Eakins'? The answer is to be found in two areas: first, the provenance, and second, the quality and relevance. A number of the photographs are signed by the artist himself, and the overwhelming majority have come from his immediate family or from two pupils, Samuel Murray or Charles Bregler. These were known to be Eakins photographs by direct, word-of-mouth statements from many who had no visible motivation for anything but the truth. Many of the photographs, chiefly those in public collections, have been subjected to the test of connoisseurship for years. If there is error, I hope that I have at least stimulated study.

Gordon Hendricks
New York, December 1969

Thomas Eakins: *His Photographic Works*

A discovery showing a close link between the paintings of Thomas Eakins, often called America's greatest painter, and photographs he himself took ranks as a major advance in our knowledge of these two arts and in the history of art itself.

In Eakins' time, few painters would admit to the use of photographs as aids to their work. Many, indeed, scorned such a device as beneath the dignity of their art. Since Daguerre's discovery in 1839, artists' mainstay, portraiture, had been dealt a severe, even fatal, blow. Although many sitters still preferred paintings to photographs because photographs were too small, the knell had been sounded, and critics everywhere agreed that painters must look elsewhere if they were to survive. Survive of course they did, and healthily, in Impressionism, Post-Impressionism, Expressionism, *et al.* In the 1880s, the period of most of Eakins' photographs, the struggle against photography was still vigorous enough to make those few painters who confessed to its use the victims of condescension.

But Eakins went about his quiet way, taking unto himself and into himself anything he felt might help his work. In Philadelphia he was surrounded by photographic amateurs of considerable reputation, although of conventional taste. The Philadelphia élite had taken the new pastime—and the new art—to its breast, and no Philadelphian needed to feel ashamed to become involved in it. It was still unconventional for a painter to espouse the cause, but what else would one expect from the man who produced the monstrous *Gross Clinic* or the "absolutely colorless" *William Rush* painting? But with photography as with dissection (for which the painter had to gird himself each new season at the Academy) Thomas Eakins used whatever means was at hand to do his work. Photography, it has now been established, was important in that work. Newly-found photographs, in fact, suggest that in Eakins' work more than in that of any other American painter, photography played a significant role.

All of this is not merely coincidence. Photography, in its uncompromising honesty, had an especial appeal for a painter who was himself uncompromisingly honest. So uncompromising, in fact, that he was rejected again and again by friend and foe alike. A photograph is a document of life as it is; Eakins' work, as his friend Walt Whitman said, is again "not a remaking of life, but life. . .just as it is."

Photographs in this exhibition indicate that Eakins sometimes went so far as to copy, brush stroke by brush stroke, from a photograph. Others demonstrate that substantial parts of finished paintings were copied directly from photographs. Still others seem to be the inspiration for works which themselves were not copies of photographs in part or in whole.

13

Fig. 1.   70.   Photographer unknown. Eakins' camera,
lenses, plate holders, carrying case and
palette. c. 1880+ Collection of
Gordon Hendricks, New York.

Fig. 2.   5.   Eakins. Margaret Eakins and "Harry."
Squan, New Jersey. 1880. Collection of
Gordon Hendricks, New York.

If Thomas Eakins had kept a diary we might know when he began to take photographs. But he did not, and we must rely on conjecture for an answer to that question. His first clearly-dated photographs were taken in the summer of 1880, the year in which the camera he used first became popular. By the beginning of 1883, according to his own statement, he had taken "many photographs and photographic studies."

The camera was a 4" x 5" American Optical Company box that began to rival in popularity the same company's 5" x 8" model only at the beginning of the decade (Number 70; Fig. 1). The Eakins-Macdowell excursion to the Jersey shore in the summer of 1880 is a logical try-out for a new camera. (To try to assign naiveté to Eakins' early photographs is difficult with a photographer who always showed a highly developed framing sense.) Finally, in addition to "many photographs and photographic studies" in Eakins' possession at the beginning of 1883, he had an accumulation of accoutrements—two additional lenses, chemicals, a solar camera, and many "accessories" (Fig. 1). Such a collection must have been the result of needs that arose from use of what he had.

He must have bought the camera with the idea of taking pictures of *people* and decided later that he wanted to take an occasional landscape or "view" as they were called. A 4" x 5" camera was just right for photographs of people, generally half-length or bust shots, and many of the artist's photographs are of this sort. Many show remarkable psychological penetration—a quality we would expect from an Eakins photograph—and suggest that it was principally for this purpose that he acquired the camera in the first place.

Eakins made a careful distinction between "photographs" and "photographic studies," and poses a delicious question: Did he regard "photographs" as ends in themselves and "studies" as means to ends, perhaps paintings? There is no doubt that a number of the photographs in this exhibition stand firmly by themselves as excellent photographs. In addition, a number of the photographic portraits, including the series of his sister Caroline in the side yard of the house and the series of his Aunt Eliza Cowperthwaite, appear to have been made with no thought of later development into paintings. "If you won't let me paint your portrait, Aunt Eliza, you'll at least let me take your picture."

THE FIRST PHOTOGRAPHS

Trips to the Jersey shore near what was then called Squan—now Manasquan and Point Pleasant—had been favorite outings for Eakins' friends and perhaps for the Eakinses themselves for some time before the 1880 excursion was made. The Philadelphia élite, including such names as Biddle, Drexel, Claghorn, Lippincott, Wilsatch, Cassatt, Childs, and, in 1877, Eakins' old friend Dr. Samuel David Gross, generally visited Spring Lake (the Monmouth House) or Sea Girt (the Beach House). These gentlemen and their families took a Pullman from downtown Philadelphia and did not even slow down at Squan. But the Macdowells, Eakins' in-laws-to-be, and other friends took the ferry to Camden and Jersey Central coach trains to their destination. This was generally the Arnold House in Point Pleasant or the Union House in what is now Brielle. "The arrivals at the Union House are. . . W.H. Macdowell and wife, Miss Dollie Macdowell, Miss Lizzie Macdowell, Phila.," an 1878 newspaper reported. Two years later what may have been a party of six young people, including Macdowells and Eakinses—and Eakins himself—made the trip and Eakins gave his camera a try-out. Five photographs taken on this happy occasion have come down to us, and three are in the exhibition.

One of these gives us our first instance of the artist's unhesitating use of different framings of the same negative. He decided that the interest in Number 19 lay chiefly in the footsteps on the beach and the shoreline itself, and accordingly he cut out much of the sky (Number 18). The tidal sand dune in Number 6 may have been where he asked his sister Margaret to stand for her picture (Number 5; Fig. 2). She posed with "Harry," the first of several setter dogs in the family, who gave the photograph a dark accent and a lower angle of a triangle silhouetted against ocean and sky.

THE ARTIST AND HIS ANIMALS

From the beginning to the end of his life Eakins liked animals—cats, dogs, horses, even monkeys. Of the dogs in his life there were "Nance," "Dinah," "Piero" and "Harry"—and chiefly "Harry." "Harry" lived to be 16 or 18 years old until he could scarcely move. He was near the end of his life when a photograph of Eakins, Samuel Murray and William O'Donovan was taken, and he was very old when the affectionate Number 137 was taken this time by Eakins himself.

The artist also frequently posed "Harry" with his wife and members of his family. In two exhibition numbers, Number 138 and Number 139, his sister Margaret is atop "Harry's" kennel, and in Number 140, on apparently the same occasion, Margaret is seated with "Harry" half in her lap. (The photographs showing the two atop the kennel are different framings of the same negative.) Margaret is also seen in a delightful photograph taken of her and "Harry" on a slight eminence beside the Mt. Vernon Street house (Number 86; Fig. 3). "Harry" was also posed with a setter friend in the yard at Mt. Vernon Street (Number 141), and in one of the exhibition's most charming pictures "Harry" is in Susan Macdowell's lap (Number 3; Fig. 4).

Everyone who visited the Eakins house at 1729 Mt. Vernon Street remembered it as being filled with cats. If you liked cats you were happy; if you did not, you were not. Eakins delighted in cat movements and in two photographs in the exhibition succeeded in making us understand something of the lithe, sensuous beauty of these movements. In one (Number 145) his cats are still, placidly (?) regarding the photographer, but in the other (Number 144), two of the *dramatis personae* are immensely preoccupied with one another while a third lies in the winter sun, blissfully indifferent.

Another cat, likely of a later time, stands on its hind feet (Number 102; Fig. 5).

THE ARTIST AND HIS FAMILY

Of all the people in Eakins' world, none had a stronger hold or a serener influence than his father Benjamin. A loving parent and a dear teacher for many years, he was also a tower of strength in the turmoil that beset the artist. An early *carte de visite* is in the exhibition (Number 44) along with a *carte* of Eakins' mother (Number 45). Two photographs taken at about the same time, in the side yard on Mt. Vernon Street, are also in the exhibition (Number 99, Fig. 6; Number 100, Fig. 7). In the second of the two, the sitter was posed in the celebrated Victorian revival chair used in so many of his son's portraits.

In the last decade of Benjamin Eakins' life, his son Tom and Tom's favorite pupil Samuel Murray often used to go bicycling together. On one of these threesomes Eakins took a photograph showing his father and Murray and his own empty bicycle (Number 12).

Fig. 3.   86.   Eakins. Margaret Eakins and "Harry."
Mount Vernon Street yard. Collection
of Gordon Hendricks, New York.

Fig. 4.   3.   Eakins. Mrs. Thomas Eakins and "Harry."
Collection of Gordon Hendricks, New York.

17

Fig. 5.   102.   Eakins. Cat. Collection of Joseph
Hirshhorn, New York.

Fig. 6.   99.   Eakins. Benjamin Eakins in Mount Vernon
Street yard. Collection of Mr. and Mrs.
Daniel W. Dietrich, II, Philadelphia.

Fig. 7. 100. Eakins. Benjamin Eakins in Mount Vernon
Street yard. Collection of Mr. and
Mrs. Daniel W. Dietrich, II, Philadelphia.

Fig. 8. 84. Eakins. W.H. Macdowell, Margaret Eakins
and two boys at Clinch Mountain. c. 1881.
Collection of The Metropolitan Museum of
Art, Gift of Charles Bregler, 1941.

Eakins' brother-in-law-to-be, William G. Macdowell, went to southwestern Virginia to seek his fortune, and the Macdowells who stayed in Philadelphia, William's father and mother, W.H. and his wife, and his sisters Dollie (Mary), Lizzie (Elizabeth) and Sue (Hannah Susan*) often went to visit him. On at least one trip Eakins and his sister Margaret also went with them, and, while there, accompanied W.H. Macdowell on a further excursion to the town of Saltville, 14 miles southwest of Marion in the southwestern corner of the state. There, among the rocky walls of Clinch Mountain, Eakins' camera caught his sister in the only one of many photographs in which she seemed to be enjoying herself (Number 84; Fig. 8).

Certainly she was not enjoying herself in a series of portraits intended for vignettes (Number 134). Possibly after Margaret's death at the end of 1882 her brother made transparencies of this photograph, of which one of two known is in the exhibition (Number 45A). The sitter is dour to the point of sullenness. Her brother, on the same occasion, in his eagerness to get a portrait that was not too unflattering, masked a negative in quarters and took a series of four more shots (Number 135). But he had met his match. He was able, in more than one painting of his sister, to achieve a kind of beauty—not to say psychological penetration. But in Margaret's photographs he came as near to failure as he ever did: he was unable to show an "inner beauty." A half-length photograph is similarly uncomplimentary (Number 68; Fig. 9), and a photograph of Margaret in his studio—one of only two known of the studio—is less a portrait than a "view" (Number 69; Fig. 10).

If his father was a confidant and a shoulder to lean upon, Margaret his greatest concern and—for that reason?—his favorite, Eakins' sister Frances and her family of young children and their farm were a place of refreshment. Early in the 1870s Frances had moved to Avondale, Pennsylvania, with her new husband, W.J. Crowell, to whose sister Eakins had

*Eakins' wife, née Hannah Susan Macdowell, is generally called "Susan Hannah," with the "h" sometimes left off. But Mrs. Eakins' own entry in the family bible gives "Hannah Susan."

Fig. 9.   68.   Eakins. Margaret Eakins. Mount Vernon Street. Collection of Gordon Hendricks, New York.

20

Fig. 10.   69.   Eakins. Margaret Eakins in Eakins' Mount
Vernon Street studio. Collection of
Gordon Hendricks, New York.

Fig. 11.   85.   Eakins. Margaret Eakins and Elizabeth
Macdowell at the farm in Avondale. Collection of Gordon Hendricks, New York.

once been engaged. Crowell had been trained for law but found the bucolic reaches of Chester County more congenial. Frances had one baby after another—Ella, Margaret, Ben and Will. And by the time Uncle Tom had taken up photography in earnest, another boy, Artie, was on the way.

It was Artie who was the center of interest for his Uncle Tom in one of the earliest photographs we have in the Avondale series. Margaret Eakins is at the left and Susan Macdowell at the right, showing a year-old Artie the inner wonders of a dandelion in a photograph full of light and springtime (Number 124). Perhaps the following autumn Margaret went out to the farm again, this time with Elizabeth Macdowell, and her brother took their photograph beside one of the great trees lining the brook down the slope behind the house (Number 85; Fig. 11). By September of 1883 another boy had arrived. This one was named after his Uncle Tom, and the proud uncle photographed the new baby, his mother, his brother Artie and Susan Macdowell, and, just beyond the lens field, "Harry." It is late summer, and the great beech tree just in range upper left casts only a wan shadow (Number 125).

The beech itself came in for a magnificent photograph of its own (Number 183). Unidentified adults make a cluster of white beneath it, and a boy and a girl, possibly niece Margaret and nephew Ben, are engaged in conversation at the right.

At this time in September of 1883, with his *Arcadia* series much on his mind, Eakins took several pictures of his young nieces and nephews, nude, in the grass along the banks of the brook. Two of these, one of Artie and an unidentified girl—no Crowell girl was the right age (Number 185)—and another of a bashful Artie (Number 186) are in the exhibition. A third photograph in this nude group is of his fiancée Susan Macdowell, with her skirts hitched up to her knees, playing with several of the children in the brook (Number 61; Fig. 12). A soft-focus halo surrounds the whole and gives an ethereal, Renoir-like sense of unreality to the proceedings.

Fig. 12. 61. Eakins. Susan Macdowell and the Crowell children on the farm in Avondale. Collection of Gordon Hendricks, New York.

Fig. 13.   66.   Eakins. Two of the artist's nephews at the
farm in Avondale. Collection of
Gordon Hendricks, New York.

Fig. 14.   65.   Eakins. Two of the artist's nephews at the
farm in Avondale. Collection of
Gordon Hendricks, New York.

In perhaps 1888 Eakins took a photograph of his brother-in-law, W.J. Crowell, with two new members of the family, a new daughter, Kathryn,* and a new dog, "Piero" (Number 126). Eakins must have used his portrait lens for this photograph, since there is a shallow depth of field. Number 126 is a print from the whole negative; a cropped enlargement is also in the exhibition (Number 126A).

The pool near the great beech was the setting for a delightful photograph of two of Eakins' young nephews. Either of the two could be Ben, Will, Artie or Tom (Number 66; Fig. 13). Here the edge of the water is in the center of the picture, so if the picture is turned upside down, only the lessened sharpness reveals that fact. In a different negative, but with the boys in an almost incredibly similar pose, Eakins made a print that amounts to an enlarged detail of this photograph (Number 65; Fig. 14). Two of the boys were also placed at the roots of a great tree, possibly the same tree as in Number 85, and photographed again (Number 60; Fig. 15).

One of the nephews, possibly Ben, was taken in a full-length side view at this time in a photograph full of the freedom and beauty of youth (Number 63; Fig. 16).

In two photographs of his sister Frances on the farmhouse steps with children, Eakins commented upon the joy and beauty of motherhood. One of these shows his sister with (from the left) Katie, Jim and Frances (Number 90; Fig. 17), and the other shows her with two of the boys and another baby, possibly Katie, at an earlier date (Number 91; Fig. 18). It is also probably Katie whose dark figure is caught in a single ray of sunlight with her doll, close in time to Number 90 (Number 62; Fig. 19).

Numbers 90 and 62 were taken at or near the time of the best-known of all Eakins' photographs of his sister Frances and her family. That photograph shows the entire family seated on the steps of the porch of the farmhouse in the spring or early summer of 1890 (the baby in Frances' lap was born in January 1890). This is exhibition Number 89; Fig. 20. "Piero" the dog is in front, and on the first step, from the left, are Artie, Ben and Will.* Will

*I do not know if this child's name was spelled "Catherine" or "Kathryn." She was known as "Katie."

Fig. 15.   60.   Eakins. Two of the artist's young relatives
at the farm in Avondale. Collection of
Gordon Hendricks, New York.

Fig. 16.   63.   Eakins. Ben Crowell? Collection of
                   Gordon Hendricks, New York.

Fig. 17.   90.   Eakins. Frances Eakins Crowell and, from
                   the left, Katie, James W. and Frances
                   Crowell. Farm in Avondale. Collection
                   of Gordon Hendricks, New York.

Fig. 18. 91. Eakins. Frances Eakins Crowell and three
of her children. Collection of Gordon
Hendricks, New York.

Fig. 19. 62. Eakins. The artist's niece, Katie Crowell,
at the farm in Avondale. Collection of
Gordon Hendricks, New York.

Fig. 20.   89.   Eakins. Frances Eakins Crowell and, from
the left, on the first step, Artie, Ben, and
Will; Margaret or Ella (Eleanor) on the
second step; W.J. Crowell and Katie on the
third step; Jim, Margaret or Ella and Tom on
the fourth step. At the farm in Avondale. Collection of The Metropolitan Museum of Art,
Gift of Charles Bregler, 1944.

Fig. 21.   88.   Eakins. Caroline Eakins with a dog. Collection of Gordon Hendricks, New York.

is holding a cat. Margaret or Ella (Eleanor) is on the second step at the right; W.J. Crowell and Katie are on the third; Jim, with a blurred face, is on the fourth step with Margaret or Ella. Tom and Mrs. W.J. Crowell holding the baby Frances are on the fourth step. The *mise en scene* is not quite a Saturnalia, with only Ben venturing a grin, and on only one side of his mouth at that.

W.J. Crowell had been told by his fiancée's father, Benjamin Eakins, that he would have to finish law school before he could marry Frances. He promptly agreed, but instead of going into practice, he bought the farm and proceeded vigorously, not to farm, but to raise a family. One of his brother-in-law's photographs suggests a certain carelessness about barnyard order (Number 162), but the aspect of the hills beyond the barnyard is more sprightly in the photograph of "Augustus" (Number 143).

Also in the exhibition is a series of photographs of Eakins' sister Caroline. Like many other photographs in the exhibition, they are previously unknown. Caroline married her brother's *bête noir,* Frank Stephens** (Number 39) and became estranged from Eakins. But at the time of this series, all was sunlight and happiness. A *carte* of Caroline at the age of 15 (Number 42A) and a tintype of Caroline with Frances and two of Frances' children (Number 42) are also in the exhibition.

*The Metropolitan Museum of Art's 1968 calendar, *Four Victorian Photographers,* identifies Will as the boy leaning against the pillar. But age and physiognomy—I have seen other photographs and met Will—suggest that Will is down front.

**Eakins gave much of the blame for the violent Academy rupture to his brother-in-law, Frank Stephens. He wrote Emily Sartain that Stephens had acquired a list of girl students who had modeled for Eakins in the nude, and boasted of his ability to have Eakins dismissed from the Academy—and Philadelphia itself.

Fig. 22. 87. Eakins. Caroline Eakins. Collection of Gordon Hendricks, New York.

Fig. 23. 67. Eakins. Tom Crowell. Collection of Gordon Hendricks, New York.

Fig. 24. 97. Eakins. Crowell farm hand? Collection of Gordon Hendricks, New York.

The five photographs of Caroline in the yard at 1729 Mt. Vernon Street may have been Eakin's first conscious attempt to take a fine photograph *per se*, without regard to a posssible later usage in his painting. Whatever his intention, he achieved photographs that stand by themselves as artistic accomplishments. Caroline's age, possibly about seventeen, suggests the summer of 1880 as an appropriate date for the series. In one photograph she is with a dog and the near-meridian sun makes a bold contrast between the two halves of the photograph (Number 88; Fig. 21); in a second she is seated with a cluster of flowers in her lap (Number 128); in a third she holds a sun shade over her head, and the photographer shows his skill with exposures by giving just the correct degree of shadow to her face (Number 87; Fig. 22); in a fourth she leans over to pat the dog (Number 130); in the fifth she stands with head bowed, a fan and a light shoulder-wrap in her hand (Number 131).

Eakins' sister Caroline was also photographed in front of the light screen—fingers can be seen on each side—with the intention being another close-up or vignette (Number 133). And in the last of the photographs of Caroline, Eakins' sister, now a young matron, is seated on a porch, possibly at Frances' farm, with a baby and a black kitten on her lap (Number 132).

One day when Ella or Margaret Crowell visited the Mt. Vernon Street house, Uncle Tom posed the child in a chair before a dark drop and caught the lugubrious expression of Number 129. Ella's brother Tom also visited the house, and his uncle caught an even more doleful expression. This is a photograph of a boy who hates to have his picture taken and is angry at being compelled to sit pushed up against the grape leaves for what he thinks is no good reason (Number 67; Fig. 23).

Eakins also photographed three Negroes, of whom two I believe were domestic servants in his father's or his sister Frances' household. One is a profile of a young male full of the directness that distinguishes the artist's work, making this one of the strongest portraits in the exhibition (Number 97; Fig. 24), another of "Old Margaret" with her head in a soft-focus halo (Number 98; Fig. 25), and a third possibly of a model.

Sometime near the middle of the 1870s Eakins met Hannah Susan Macdowell. Susan was in Eakins' Academy classes as early as 1877, and it was not long before the two were on friendly terms. A photograph of a tintype by the City Gallery of Philadelphia shows Miss Macdowell as she must have been at about the time she met Eakins (Number 10). Not as dour as the Crowells, she nevertheless is not a picture of bubbling good spirits. Eakins photographed his wife-to-be for a vignette, although in this case only the vignette—and not the whole print—remains (Number 1; Fig. 26).

Another photograph, taken some years later, shows her in an equally dispirited mood (Number 4) as does a much later photograph in her late thirties (Number 8) and a theatrical-looking photograph as a lady at the beginning of old-age (Number 7; Fig. 27).

But a prize in the collection, a blue print, shows Susan Macdowell as she must have looked as a bride, with vibrant life, gentleness and love lighting up her face (Number 2; Fig. 28).

Two other photographs show Mrs. Eakins as she was at about this age, and as she must often have posed for her husband and teacher, in the nude. The first shows her with "Harry" in the Mt. Vernon Street yard (see earlier Number 3; Fig. 4) and the other is Number 9. Thirty years or so later, when Mrs. Eakins was sixty or more, her husband's pupil Samuel Murray

Fig. 25. 98. Eakins. "Old Margaret." Eakins'(?) servant.
Collection of Gordon Hendricks, New York.

Fig. 26. 1. Eakins, Susan Macdowell. Collection of
Walter Macdowell, Roanoke, Va.

Fig. 27.   7.   Eakins. Mrs. Thomas Eakins. Collection
of Walter Macdowell, Roanoke, Va.

Fig. 28.   2.   Eakins. Susan Macdowell Eakins. c. 1884.
Collection of Walter Macdowell,
Roanoke, Va.

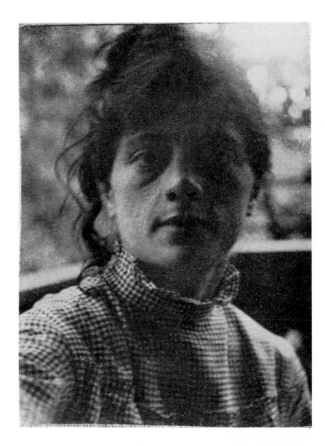

Fig. 29. 11. Murray. Susan Macdowell Eakins in Mount
Vernon Street yard. c. 1914. Collection
of Walter Macdowell, Roanoke, Va.

Fig. 31. 78. Eakins. Mrs. William H. Macdowell. Mount
Vernon Street yard. Collection of
Gordon Hendricks, New York.

Fig. 32. 80. Eakins. William H. Macdowell. Detail of
Number 78; Fig. 31. Collection of The
Metropolitan Museum of Art, David Hunter
McAlpin Fund, 1943.

Fig. 33. 76. Eakins. William H. Macdowell. Race Street
porch? Collection of Mr. and Mrs.
Daniel W. Dietrich, II, Philadelphia.

Fig. 34 193. Eakins. William H. Macdowell. Detail of
Number 76; Fig. 33. Collection of The
Metropolitan Museum of Art,
David Hunter McAlpin Fund, 1943.

visited the house and took a series of pictures in the side yard. In one of these Mrs. Eakins stooped down to embrace a brace of cats, looked up, and was caught by Murray's camera in a happy mood (Number 11; Fig. 29). Mrs. Eakins had this photograph printed on a postcard and sent it to relatives and friends with "Our Family" written on it.

Two photographs of William H. Macdowell, Susan's father, were intended as vignettes or other details. In Number 78 (Fig. 31) Eakins printed the whole negative, and in Number 80 (Fig. 32) he excluded Macdowell's feet and the legs of the chair in which he sat. Another of Macdowell (Number 76; Fig. 33) was treated the same way (Number 193; Fig. 34). The Macdowells lived not far away from the Eakinses at 2016 Race Street and their son-in-law caught W.H. and his wife on the porch with Macdowell looking like an Appalachian Jeremiah (Number 56; Fig. 35). Eakins may have made a larger negative of another W.H. Macdowell pose (Number 75; Fig. 36), but if he did the larger version, of which the exhibition photograph might be a detail, has not come down to us.

On another occasion, perhaps in one of the studios in the Mt. Vernon Street house, Eakins photographed Mrs. Macdowell in a boldly-lighted, direct portrait (Number 77; Fig. 37).

Another in the collection of in-laws' photographs in the exhibition is a full-shot of Mary (Dollie) Macdowell, the companion of Jersey shore days (Number 57). Unusual in this photograph is evidence of spotting. Either Eakins, or another, later printer, thought the face was too dark, and so he held back light from that part of the print with the result that Miss Macdowell's face and the upper part of her body are brighter than they were in nature. If this was done by Eakins it is the only occasion I know of in which he manipulated a print.

On another occasion Eakins sat his brother-in-law William G. Macdowell before the screen in the yard, printed the full negative (Number 206) and made a vignette of it (Number 207). The result is a portrait of a strong-jawed, strong-willed man, according to family legend and the evidence of Eakins' photograph, "a lady-killer."

A photograph of Elizabeth Macdowell in the Mt. Vernon Street yard, in a pose reminiscent of the series of Caroline, rounds out Eakins' records of his in-laws (Number 179).

THE ARTIST AND THE ACADEMY

When the Pennsylvania Academy of the Fine Arts opened in its new building in 1876, Eakins was hired to help out the aging Christian Schuessele in his classes. Before the first year was out he had had a row with the directors and was gone. But he was soon back—at the directors' urging—and stayed an uninterrupted nine years. During this tenure a number of photographs were taken of his classes, apparently by Eakins himself, and six of these are in the exhibition. Two are informal, crowded and unposed: in one of these Eakins' students are gathered around the skeleton of a horse, on which is fixed the skeleton of a rider (Number 155), and in the other a smaller group is tightly packed into a patch of sunlight with no attempt to identify themselves with an art school (Number 200). Another shows the women's modeling class with Blanche Hurlbut, whose portrait by Eakins is in the Philadelphia Museum of Art, seated on the floor at the left (Number 73; Fig. 38); a later view (now a series of little cows range themselves along the case at the back) shows a similar class in a somewhat sillier mood (Number 156). Another shows a mixed class modeling from a live horse—one of the things that began to get on the Academy authorities' nerves. Like others in the exhibition, this photograph is here attributed to Eakins for the first time

Fig. 35. 56. Eakins. Mr. and Mrs. William H. Macdowell
on porch of their Race Street house.
Collection of Walter Macdowell, Roanoke, Va.

Fig. 36. 75. Eakins. William H. Macdowell. Mount
Vernon Street yard. Collection of
Gordon Hendricks, New York.

(Number 154). The most formal of the group of six showing Academy students is a photograph of possibly one section of the antique class with Adam Emory Albright, father of Ivan and Zsissly Albright, at the right in the front row (Number 153).

One day in the early 1880s Eakins took a number of his men students to a secluded place and took a number of photographs showing the men, nude, wrestling. Although they appear to be enjoying themselves, their joy is not entirely uninhibited. They are glad, in their devotion to their teacher, to do as he says, but they cannot help being self-conscious about it (Number 159).

When the Philadelphia Art Students League was formed by Eakins' students immediately after Eakins left the Academy, and Eakins volunteered to teach its classes, a new young student from New York City, Franklin Schenck, soon became what was euphemistically called "curator" of the new League. Actually, Schenck acted as janitor, keeping the stove, cleaning the place, and living there. In an Eakins photograph showing Schenck in the studio, Schenck is hunched over with his hands on his knees above a tug-of-war apparatus used by the students to keep in shape (Number 203). On the wall behind him are a dozen palettes, four photographs—apparently of a nude woman—a clock and a clothes' rack. In the rear is the stove that Schenck tended. Eakins also photographed Schenck in the nude standing beside a brown horse (Number 15). This may have been at the Avondale farm where Schenck was remembered by the Crowell children as a frequent, welcome visitor. Other League students served as models for their fellows, one photograph showing Charles Brinton Cox, the sculptor, drawing a male nude (Number 204) and a second shows a female nude, possibly not a student, reclining in front of a screen (Number 205).

Weda Cook of *Concert Singer* fame (Number 213; Fig. 39) was a frequent visitor to the boys in the newly-formed League. Her warm personality, as well as her singing, must have been a great encouragement at the times when their realization that they had cut themselves off from "official" Philadelphia art had a particularly cold clutch. Eakins' photographs of Weda Cook show this affection. A group of three photographs in the exhibition show Weda in what are loosely called "Greek" robes. In one of these she is alone in a full profile (Number 165); in another she is full-face with the League's classic plaster at her side (Number 164; Fig. 40); in a third she is with her sisters Kathryn and Dorothy in a grouping showing Eakins' power in arranging figures (Number 166). A fourth member of this "Greek" group shows Kathryn Cook with the torso (Number 163).

Eakins loved sailing, a feeling he managed to get into another photograph in the exhibition—along with a subtle feeling of surrealism (Number 96; Fig. 41). This could have been taken on the Delaware shore, south of Gloucester, at the rim of the marshes to which sailing Philadelphians, including Eakins, eagerly repaired in quest of their favorite game, rail and reed-birds.

"A LITTLE TRIP TO THE WEST"

To renew his spirit as well as his body after the harrowing rupture with the Academy, Eakins betook himself to the Little Badlands of North Dakota in July of 1887. "I am going to take a little trip to the West," he wrote. While staying there he visited two ranches, both some distance north of Medora, North Dakota. Here he took three of the photographs in the exhibition: one of a cowboy in full regalia outside a ranch house (Number 187), another of perhaps the ranch owner's wife astride a white pony (Number 188), and a third of a horse

Fig. 37. 77. Eakins. Mrs. William H. Macdowell. Collection of The Metropolitan Museum of Art, Gift of Charles Bregler.

Fig. 38. 73. Eakins. Women's modeling class at the Academy. Blanche Hurlbut seated on the floor at left. c. 1885. Collection of The Metropolitan Museum of Art, Gift of Charles Bregler.

Fig. 39.   213.   Eakins. *The Concert Singer*, 1892. Oil on canvas. Collection of the Philadelphia Museum of Art.

Fig. 40.   164.   Eakins. Weda Cook with Academy plaster cast. Collection of Gordon Hendricks, New York.

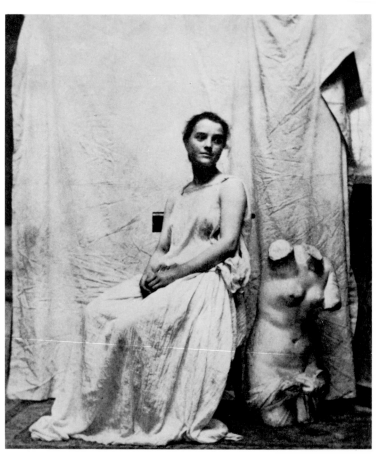

Fig. 41. 96. Eakins. Sailboats. Delaware River? Collection of the Philadelphia Museum of Art.

Fig. 42. 210. Eakins. *Amelia Van Buren*, 1891. Oil on canvas. Collection of the Phillips Collection, Washington, D.C.

Fig. 43.   58.   Eakins. Amelia C. Van Buren. c. 1891.
Collection of the Philadelphia Museum of Art.

Fig. 44.   59.   Eakins. Amelia Van Buren. c. 1891. Collection of Mr. and Mrs. Daniel W. Dietrich, II,
Philadelphia.

Fig. 45. 110. Eakins. Walt Whitman. First floor sitting room in Whitman's Camden house. Collection of Yale University, New Haven, Connecticut.

Fig. 46. 112. Eakins. Walt Whitman. Second floor bedroom in Whitman's Camden house. Collection of the Philadelphia Museum of Art.

and a dog (Number 142). It is not certain that the last photograph is western, particularly since the wooded terrain in the background is unlike the Little Badlands country. But since the pony is western and the rifle slung alongside is western, and the dog is unknown, the evidence is toward the Dakota trip.

THE ARTIST AND WALT WHITMAN

Shortly after he got back from Dakota, Eakins went with his friend Talcott Williams to meet Walt Whitman in Camden. Eakins and Whitman immediately hit it off, and soon Eakins was at work on a portrait of Whitman (Number 113). Whitman liked the portrait very much and stuck to it, as he said, "like molasses holds on to the jug."

Whitman was impatient with photographers. He had been "photographed, photographed, and photographed," he said, "until the cameras themselves are tired of me. . . No man has been photographed more than I have or photographed worse: I've run the whole gamut of photographic fol-de-rol." But he liked Eakins, and he did not mind Eakins taking pictures of him. Of eight photographs now extant which I believe were taken by Eakins, four are in the exhibition, and three of these are reproduced in the catalogue. The earliest shows Whitman as he was at the time the portrait was being planned (Number 110; Fig. 45); another shows him at the window of his second floor bedroom in Camden with a wolf-skin flung over the back of his chair (Number 112; Fig. 46); a third and a fourth show him as he was near death, propped up in a chair and are the last photographs taken of this much-photographed man (Number 111, Fig. 47; Number 114). Numbers 112 and 114 have been attributed to Eakins' friend and pupil Samuel Murray, but this is incorrect.

Eakins' portrait of Whitman, as well as a sketch for the portrait (Number 115; Fig. 48), show little or no use of photographs.

Fig. 47.   111.   Eakins. Walt Whitman. Second floor bedroom
in Whitman's Camden house. 1891. Collec-
tion of the Philadelphia Museum of Art.

Fig. 48.   115.   Eakins. *Walt Whitman*, c. 1887. Oil on wo●
sketch for Number 113. Collection of the
Boston Museum of Fine Arts, Helen
and Alice Colburn Fund.

Fig. 49. 209. Eakins. *Frank St. John*, 1900. Oil on canvas.
Collection of Kennedy Galleries, New York.

Fig. 50. 50. Eakins. Samuel Murray at work on his bust
of Frank St. John. Collection of Mr. and
Mrs. Daniel W. Dietrich, II, Philadelphia.

Fig. 51. 49. Eakins. Samuel Murray with his bust of
Franklin Schenck. 1330 Chestnut Street
studio. c. 1890. Collection of the Philadelphia Museum of Art.

Fig. 52. 109. Eakins. George W. Holmes, blind painter
and teacher. Collection of The Metro-
politan Museum of Art, David Hunter
McAlpin Fund, 1943.

Fig. 53. 103. Eakins. Mrs. Anna Kershaw. Collection of Joseph Hirshhorn, New York.

Fig. 54. 104. Eakins? Jennie Dean Kershaw (later Mrs. Samuel Murray). 1330 Chestnut Street studio? Collection of Joseph Hirshhorn, New York.

Among the many unknown Eakins photographs in the exhibition are three showing the striking physiognomy of his pupil Amelia Van Buren, of whom he did a remarkable portrait, now in the Phillips Gallery (Number 210; Fig. 42). One of the new ones is a horizontal composition and includes a cat (Number 58; Fig. 43). It was obviously taken on the same occasion as the well-known one of Miss Van Buren in the Metropolitan Museum of Art (Number 117). Another new photograph shows the sitter before the same tapestry backdrop but in a somewhat theatrical chair which suggests neither 1729 Mt. Vernon Street or 1330 Chestnut where Eakins had a studio for many years (Number 59; Fig. 44). These Van Buren photographs appear to have been taken at about the same time as the celebrated c.1891 portrait by Eakins.

It was at the studio Eakins shared with Murray that another photograph was taken which shows Eakins' unhesitating use of cropping. A nude man, said to have been a great athlete (considering the stomach, a curious fact) who died shortly after this photograph was taken, is seated in front of a cloth curtain (Number 201). Until recently, when this print was presented to the Philadelphia Museum, it was thought that the Metropolitan's version of this work was the only one existing (Number 202).

In 1900, in the same studio, Eakins painted Frank St. John (Number 209; Fig. 49) and Murray photographed the sitting (Number 172). Murray also sculpted St. John at the same time. One day while Murray was at work on the bust his "dear Master" photographed him (Number 50; Fig. 50). Murray's bust of Benjamin Eakins is at the left, and at the right, on

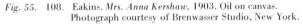

Fig. 55. 108. Eakins. *Mrs. Anna Kershaw*, 1903. Oil on canvas.
Photograph courtesy of Brenwasser Studio, New York.

Fig. 56. 107. Eakins. *Mrs. Samuel Murray*, c. 1897. Oil on canvas. Collection of F.M. Hall, University of Nebraska, Lincoln, Nebraska.

Fig. 57. 71. Eakins. Motion photograph of unidentified model. University of Pennsylvania. 1885. Collection of the Franklin Institute, Philadelphia.

the wall above the work bench, a mask I think may well be of David Wilson Jordan, another Eakins pupil and friend. Murray also sculpted Franklin Schenck, the League's curator, and Eakins took a close-up of this procedure (Number 49; Fig. 51). Eakins also photographed Murray astride a horse, nude (Number 120). The exhibition also contains another photograph of Murray, in a half-length portrait, in shirt-sleeves (Number 174).

THE ARTIST AND HIS FRIENDS

Murray's bust of George W. Holmes, the painter and teacher, was obviously directly helped by another Eakins photograph (Number 109; Fig. 52). The Murray bust is a dead ringer for the photograph (Number 169). Holmes was also photographed in the remarkable series of glass-positive nudes in the exhibition (Number 208). He is the right-hand man in Eakins' *The Chess Players*. When Eakins' photograph was taken, Holmes was blind.

During the early years of Eakins' long and close friendship with Samuel Murray, a young woman named Jennie Dean Kershaw was sometimes with them. Eakins painted both her and her mother, Mrs. Anna Kershaw, and photographed both the ladies: Anna Kershaw (Number 103, Fig. 53; Number 108, Fig. 55) and Jennie Dean (Number 104, Fig. 54; Number 107, Fig. 56; Number 175). Miss Kershaw later—considerably later, as a matter of fact, early in 1916, when Murray was forty-seven and only five months before Eakins died—became Mrs. Samuel Murray.

A camera said to be Eakins' and Murray's is in the Hirshhorn collection. This a a Number 4 cartridge Kodak, taking pictures 4" by 5", and first offered for sale in 1904, I have identified none of the photographs associated with either Eakins or Murray with this camera. The great majority of photographs identified with Eakins were taken before he met Murray, and those taken after he met Murray, such as the photograph of Murray sculpting, Schenck, etc., were taken with the 4" x 5" American Optical Company camera of c.1880.

THE ARTIST AND UNKNOWN SITTERS

Five photographs of unknown sitters are also in the exhibition. One shows a young woman and a child in an Arcadian setting (Number 182). A second is a remarkable close-up of an elderly lady, one of the rare full profiles from the artist's hand (Number 184). A third shows another elderly lady seated before the familiar white screen (Number 181). This lady, like the one immediately following, are perhaps friends or neighbors; they show no Eakins or Cowperthwaite family resemblance.* A fourth is a strong photograph of an elderly lady full of firmness, duty and devotion (Number 180A). The fifth photograph in the group of unknown sitters is of a younger woman (Number 14). This photograph is curiously captioned "Sue" in the Hirshhorn Collection.

---

*I have a *carte de visite* album containing scores of Eakins and Cowperthwaite photographs, the album kept by the Eakins family. The Eakins and Cowperthwaite "look"—particularly the Cowperthwaite—is pronounced.

Fig. 58.   54.   Eakins. *Hauling the Seine*, 1882. Oil on
canvas. Collection of Cincinnati Art Museum.

Fig. 59.   53.   Eakins. Shad fishing. Delaware River south
of Gloucester, New Jersey. c. 1882.
Collection of Gordon Hendricks, New York.

It has often been said that Eakins made a significant contribution to the development of the motion picture. This is incorrect. But what Eakins did in the line of motion photographs was important to him and his work and thus to the history of art. He achieved, incidentally, some very beautiful results. Five of his motion series photographs, all taken in the summer of 1884, are in the exhibition. The apparatus he used, a so-called Marey wheel, will be described in detail in my forthcoming book on Eakins' photography. With it he shot five of the six photographs in this group. First, the photograph of a pupil—apparently a very young one (Number 71; Fig. 57); second, a photograph of Jesse Godley, another Eakins pupil (Number 160); third, a photograph of a pole-vaulter who has been identified as George Reynolds, the subject of Eakins' portrait *The Veteran* (Number 158); fourth, a photograph which Eakins himself apparently regarded as his most attractive (Number 152); and last, a photograph that was taken of the artist himself on the 27th of August, 1884 (Number 151).

It is an interesting fact that the present exhibition may not be the first time an Eakins photograph was exhibited at the Academy. In 1886 the Photographic Society of Philadelphia held an exhibition in the Academy rooms, and one of the photographs was entitled *History of a Jump*, a most appropriate title for Number 152. It was on this photograph also that Eadweard Muybridge, "the father of the motion picture" who was then conducting his celebrated experiments at the University of Pennsylvania, wrote technical details (Number 118). And at the bottom of the print, with his "University of Pennsylvania./E," Muybridge put his seal of authenticity on the photograph.

Eakins also took photographs with another version of the Marey wheel. This time the photographic plate itself was moved behind a shutter. One of these photographs, a series of Eakins' pupil J. Laurie Wallace, is in the exhibition (Number 119).

Muybridge had published, early in 1879, a series of five cabinet-size photographs of various gaits of the horse. These he sold for $1.50 each, and many in Philadelphia, including Eakins, bought a set. The artist found them fascinating, and they were the direct inspiration and tool for *A May Morning in the Park* or *The Fairman Rogers Four-in-hand*. He used these

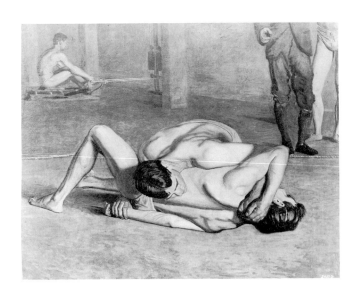

Fig. 62.   95.   Eakins. *The Wrestlers*, 1899. Oil on canvas. Collection of the National Academy of Design, New York.

Fig. 60.   55.   Eakins. *Drawing the Seine*, 1882. Watercolor.
Collection of the John G. Johnson Collec-
tion, Philadelphia.

Fig. 61.   52.   Eakins. Photograph from which the water-
color *Drawing the Seine* was taken. Timber
Creek estuary. 1882. Collection of
Gordon Hendricks, New York.

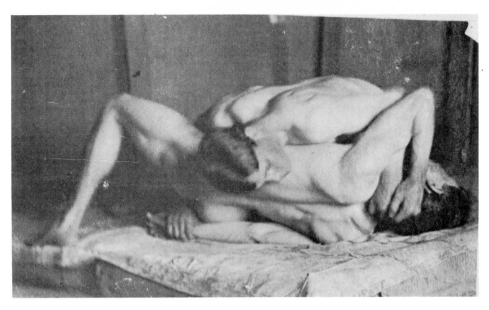

Fig. 63. 93B. Eakins. Wrestlers, top wrestler possibly
Joseph McCann. 1889? Collection of
Joseph Hirshhorn, New York.

Fig. 64. 215. Eakins. *The Swimming Hole*, 1883. Oil on
canvas. Collection of the Forth Worth Art
Center, Forth Worth, Texas.

Fig. 65. 51. Eakins. Eakins' pupils at *The Swimming Hole* site. 1883? Collection of Mr. and Mrs. Daniel W. Dietrich, II, Philadelphia.

Fig. 66. 81. Eakins. *Arcadia*, 1883. Bas-relief. New York. Collection of Joseph Hirshhorn, New York.

little Muybridge photographs for his Academy lectures; two of these slides are in the exhibition (Numbers 149 and 150). He hired one of his lady students, Ellen Wetherald Ahrens, a miniaturist, to draw the little figures on glass. Then he himself drew the trajectories and the charts at the bottom of each slide, which show the points of contact the horse's hooves have with the earth.

The only photograph Eakins took at this time of a moving horse shows that he had little success in stopping the movement. Indeed, we can scarcely be sure the horse is moving (Number 147). Another photograph of a horse standing still, which may not be Eakins', is in the exhibition. On it Eakins has drawn a number of lines showing measurements, etc. (Number 168).

In 1879, when the artist was planning his monumental work on horses in motion, *A May Morning in the Park* or *The Fairman Rogers Four-in-hand*, he visited Rogers' farm and took a photograph of his friend and patron on "Josephine," Rogers' favorite mare (Number 157).

THE ARTIST AND HIS WORK

The most illuminating and perhaps significant aspect of the recent discovery of many unknown Eakins photographs is the close relationship they demonstrate with his work. The artist thought principally in terms of *values*, not color, and the black and white of the photograph must have immediately appealed to him as a means whereby he might instantly analyze and record these values. Once recorded, he did not hesitate to use them.

Sometimes a photograph helped him to remember details of a painting, as in *Mending the Net* (Number 123) where he used a photograph of the geese in the left foreground (Number 121). At another time he used a photograph to give him the entire background for a painting, such as in *An Arcadian* (Number 197) where the trees on his sister's farm gave him all he needed (Number 196). Sometimes he used a photograph to suggest compositions as well as document them, such as in *Hauling the Seine* (Number 54; Fig. 58). For this work, Number 53; Fig. 59 may well have been useful.

In Eakins' shad-fishing series of paintings is a watercolor called *Drawing the Seine* in the Johnson Collection at the Philadelphia Museum (Number 55; Fig. 60). Nothing yet discovered in the relationship between art and photography is so specific as Eakins' use of a photograph for that work (Number 52; Fig. 61).

When Eakins was working on his *Wrestlers* (Number 95; Fig. 62) perhaps more likely, planning it, he invited a couple of the habitués of the Quaker City Athletic Club up to his Chestnut Street studio. There he took several photographs of the two in various wrestling holds. One of these photographs is in the exhibition (Number 148). Eakins must have been dissatisfied with what he saw from this series for he copied his painting, detail by detail, from another photograph (Number 93B; Fig. 63).

In *The Swimming Hole* (Number 215; Fig. 64) Eakins used photographs of the bodies in the painting (he seems to have made the faces portraits of persons not on location) and of the rocky site of the work (Number 51, Fig. 65; and Number 198).

Fig. 67. 83. Eakins. Model J. Laurie Wallace posing with pan pipes in a landscape. c. 1883. Collection of the Philadelphia Museum of Art.

Fig. 68. 191. Eakins. Girls in Greek costume. Collection of The Metropolitan Museum of Art, David Hunter McAlpin Fund, 1943.

Fig. 69.   94.   Eakins. *Arcadia,* 1883. Oil on canvas. Collection of The Metropolitan Museum of Art, bequest of Miss Adelaide Milton de Groot (1876-1967) 1967.

Fig. 71.   92B. Eakins. Reclining boy, playing pipes. Ben
Crowell? Collection of Joseph Hirshhorn,
New York.

Fig. 72.   180.   Eakins. Eliza Cowperthwaite. Collection
of Gordon Hendricks, New York.

In his bas-relief of *Arcadia* (Number 81; Fig. 66) a photograph he took of his pupil J. Laurie Wallace is closely related to the seated right-hand figure (Number 83; Fig. 67). For this work also, he may have utilized a lost member of his Greek-girl series for the center group (Number 191; Fig. 68).

In another Arcadia work, this one an oil called simply *Arcadia* (Number 94; Fig. 69), Eakins combined several photographs. The standing figure at the right is taken directly from a photograph (Number 93A); the reclining boy in the center also directly from a photograph, possibly of his nephew Ben Crowell (Number 92B; Fig. 71); the reclining female possibly from more than one photograph, for example, Number 205, with the arm (which, incidentally, looks worked-over) changed from the wrist to the elbow. The trees are reminiscent of trees along the brook in Avondale (Number 61, Fig. 12; Number 66, Fig. 13).

A photograph of J. Laurie Wallace may have been rejected (for obvious reasons) as a pose for *Arcadia* (Number 189).

Eakins produced a number of photographic portraits which will, I believe, remain as excellent photographs *per se*. Among these are those of his Aunt Eliza Cowperthwaite (Number 180; Fig. 72), the series of his sister Frances with the children, his nephews by the reflecting pond, his sister Caroline in the yard, his father-in-law, Walt Whitman, etc. But he also produced a number of photographs which he used in painting portraits. His portrait of Franklin Schenck (Number 16; Fig. 73) was clearly helped by a photograph (Number 17; Fig. 74). His portrait of Frank Hamilton Cushing (Number 105; Fig. 75) is more directly taken from a photograph (Number 106; Fig. 76). Even his portrait of Dr. Benjamin Sharpe, *The Oboe Player* (Number 194), is suggestive of a photograph that accompanied Sharpe's obituary, whether it is by Eakins or not (Number 195).

Fig. 73.   16.   Eakins. *Franklin Schenck*. c. 1890. Oil on canvas. 24" x 20." Collection of the Delaware Art Center, Society of the Fine Arts. Wilmington.

Fig. 74.   17.   Eakins. Eakins' pupil, Franklin Schenck.
c. 1890. Collection of Joseph Hirshhorn,
New York.

Fig. 75.   105.   Eakins. *Frank Hamilton Cushing*, 1895.
Oil on canvas. Collection of the Thomas
Gilcrease Institute of American History
and Art, Tulsa, Oklahoma.

Fig. 76.   106.   Eakins. Frank Hamilton Cushing. 1895.
Collection of Joseph Hirshhorn, New York.

Fig. 77. 74. Photographer unknown. Burlesque of *The Gross Clinic* with Eakins' Philadelphia Sketch Club with, possibly, Eakins at lower left. c. 1875. Collection of the Philadelphia Museum of Art.

Fig. 78. 82. J. Laurie Wallace? Thomas Eakins, 1883? Collection of The Metropolitan Museum of Art, David Hunter McAlpin Fund, 1943.

Twenty-four photographs of the artist himself have been gathered. In roughly chronological order these are: a print from a daguerreotype as a boy (Number 20); two *cartes*, one showing him as a young man with a moustache and another without (Number 41 and Number 40); a photograph showing him in a sailor suit (Number 22); a photograph showing him curled up reading in what appears to be window seat (Number 171); a photograph I believe to show Eakins and his Philadelphia Sketch Club students in a burlesque of *The Gross Clinic* (Number 74; Fig. 77) with Eakins as the horrified relative at the lower left; one of a "tormented" series, likely taken on the occasion of a need for an "official" photograph (Number 21); a photograph taken in the yard of the house, likely at a time when he had been photographing others and someone said, "Now let's take *your* photograph, Tom" (Number 23); a photograph taken for a *Harper's Monthly* article, "A Clever Town Built by Quakers," February 1882 (Number 24) and the engraving made from it (Number 25); two nude photographs, one showing Eakins playing the pipes (Number 82; Fig. 78) which must have been taken during the *Arcadia* work and another showing Eakins and J. Laurie Wallace which could have been taken at the same time (Number 190); an official-looking photograph, one of a series of three, taken in the Chestnut Street studio likely in the early 1890s (Number 31); a "candid" shot, apparently a detail of an unlocated print showing Eakins carrying an easel (?) (Number 26); another showing Eakins reclining nude (Number 31A); another photograph taken at the Avondale farm, showing him modeling a horse for the Brooklyn Memorial Arch (Number 37); another showing him with Samuel Murray and William O'Donovan seated at a table at 1330 Chestnut Street regaling themselves with what looks suspiciously like wine (Number 101); a photograph showing him looking uncomfortable in a three-piece suit, shirt and tie, hat in hand (Number 28; Fig. 79); another showing him astride his horse, also likely at Avondale (Number 36); a photograph showing him with what has been called a smile (Number 27); three photographs showing him astride "Billy," two in the nude (Numbers 34 and 35; Fig. 80) and a third showing him clothed with "Billy" moving along at a fast clip (Number 146); a photograph illustrating the wild abandon with which he enjoyed his outings on the Cohansey River with his beloved pupil Samuel Murray (Number 178); another, of 1906, showing quite the reverse (Number 29); a photograph showing him contemplating a Murray sculpture of him with pussy willows adding a melancholy note to an already too-melancholy scene (Number 30; Fig. 81); another of possibly the same time showing the artist in a customary gloomy mood (Number 170); a photograph showing him with his back turned, indistinct against the northeast window of his fourth-floor studio (Number 32); another showing Eakins' remarkable resemblance to his father, in the right background of Number 173, a photograph taken by Samuel Murray on the same occasion as the photograph of Mrs. Eakins (Number 11; Fig. 29); and finally, a photograph showing him with the last of his dogs, seated in the doorway of his house, the last of the exhibition's photographs of Thomas Eakins, photographer (Number 33; Fig. 82). Another photograph, taken on the same occasion and showing Eakins tweaking the ear of the same dog, has been called the artist's last. These two are, indeed, the last I know.

G.H.

Fig. 79.   28.   Samuel Murray. Thomas Eakins. Collection
of the Philadelphia Museum of Art.

Fig. 80.   35.   Photographer unknown. Thomas Eakins
astride "Billy." Farm in Avondale. c. 1892.
Collection of the Philadelphia Museum of Art.

Fig. 81. 30. Photographer unknown. Thomas Eakins
with Samuel Murray's sculpture of him.
Collection of Gordon Hendricks, New York.

Fig. 82. 33. Samuel Murray? Thomas Eakins in the
door of Mount Vernon Street House.
c. 1915. Collection of The Metropolitan
Museum of Art.

Where the *dramatis personae* of the exhibition's photographs is uncertain, I have omitted identification, and where dates were uncertain I have omitted an estimate. I am aware that there have been—and will continue to be—identifications and datings that do not appear on this check list. But where dating is involved I prefer to commit the sin of omission rather than that of commission. Sizes are from actual measurements of original prints by the photographer, with heights before widths. These are occasionally irregular, and where they are very irregular I have so noted. Numbers such as 146, 148, 155 and 200 are modern enlargements, chiefly by Charles Bregler, from copy negatives of unlocated prints. These unlocated prints appear themselves to have been taken from copy negatives, and we may therefore assume that the original negatives were unavailable to Bregler. Many more of such modern enlargements are in the collections of the Metropolitan and Philadelphia Museums. A few photographs, such as Numbers 90 and 137, are enlargements by Eakins himself, who rarely enlarged prints.

All the photographs in the exhibition could have been taken with the artist's 4" x 5" American Optical Company camera. And the fact that he did not buy another camera until 1904 or later and no photograph of 1904 or later has been identified with him, suggests that all the photographs were, indeed, taken with this early camera.

G. H.

Fig. 26	1.	Eakins. Susan Macdowell. 4-1/8" x 3-1/8" (10.5 cm. x 7.9 cm.) Reproduction by Rolf P. Petersen. Collection of Walter Macdowell, Roanoke, Va.
Fig. 28.	2.	Eakins. Susan Macdowell Eakins. c. 1884. 3-3/4" x 2-5/8" (9.5 cm. x 6.7 cm.) Reproduction by Rolf P. Petersen. Collection of Walter Macdowell, Roanoke, Va.
Fig. 4.	3.	Eakins. Mrs. Thomas Eakins and "Harry." 3-7/16" x 3-5/16" (8.7 cm. x 8.4 cm.) Reproduction by Rolf P. Petersen. Collection of Gordon Hendricks, New York.
	4.	Eakins. Susan Macdowell. 4-1/8" x 3-1/4" (10.3 cm. x 8.3 cm.) Reproduction by Rolf P. Petersen. Collection of Walter Macdowell, Roanoke, Va.
Fig. 2.	5.	Eakins. Margaret Eakins and "Harry." Squan, New Jersey. 1880. 4-1/8" x 3-1/8" (10.5 cm. x 8 cm.) Reproduction by Rolf P. Petersen. Collection of Gordon Hendricks, New York.
	6.	Eakins. Beach at Squan. 2-1/2" x 3-11/16" (6.4 cm. x 9.4 cm.) Reproduction by Rolf P. Petersen. Collection of Mr. and Mrs. Daniel W. Dietrich, II, Philadelphia.
Fig. 27.	7.	Eakins. Mrs. Thomas Eakins. 6-1/4" x 4-1/2" (15.9 cm. x 11.5 cm.) Reproduction by Rolf P. Petersen. Collection of Walter Macdowell, Roanoke, Va.
	8.	Eakins. Mrs. Thomas Eakins. 1-15/16" x 2" (5 cm. x 5.1 cm.) Reproduction by Rolf P. Petersen. Collection of Walter Macdowell, Roanoke, Va.
	9.	Eakins. Mrs. Thomas Eakins. Yard at Mount Vernon Street. 3-3/16" x 4-15/16" (8.1 cm. x 12.6 cm.) Reproduction by Rolf P. Petersen. Collection of Joseph Hirshhorn, New York.
	10.	Eakins. Susan Macdowell. 3-1/2" x 2-3/8" (8.9 cm. x 5.6 cm.) Reproduction by Rolf P. Petersen. Collection of Walter Macdowell, Roanoke, Va.
Fig. 29.	11.	Murray. Susan Macdowell Eakins in Mount Vernon Street yard. c. 1914. 2-13/16" x 2-1/2" (7.2 cm. x 6.4 cm.) Reproduction by Rolf P. Petersen. Collection of Walter Macdowell, Roanoke, Va.
	12.	Eakins. Samuel Murray and Benjamin Eakins with Eakins' bicycle. 5-1/16" x 6-15/16" (12.9 cm. x 17.7 cm.) Reproduction by Rolf P. Petersen. Collection of Joseph Hirshhorn, New York.
	13.	Eakins. Male, farm hand. 3-13/16" x 2-5/8" (9.7 cm. x 6.7 cm.) Reproduction by Rolf P. Petersen. Collection of Joseph Hirshhorn, New York.
	14.	Eakins. Young girl. 7-3/4" x 6" (19.7 cm. x 15.7 cm.) Reproduction by Rolf P. Petersen. Collection of Joseph Hirshhorn, New York.

15. Eakins. Schenck, nude, beside a horse. 6-1/8" x 6-15/16" (15.6 cm. x 17.7 cm.) Reproduction by William Pons. Collection of The Metropolitan Museum of Art, Gift of Charles Bregler.

Fig. 73. 16. Eakins. *Franklin Schenck*, c. 1890. Oil on canvas. 24" x 20." Photograph courtesy of the Delaware Art Center, Wilmington. Collection of the Delaware Art Center, Society of the Fine Arts, Wilmington.

Fig. 74. 17. Eakins. Eakins' pupil, Franklin Schenck. c. 1890. 4-5/8" x 3-11/16" (11.8 cm. x 9.4 cm.) Reproduction by O.E. Nelson. Collection of Joseph Hirshhorn, New York.

18. Eakins. Beach at Squan. 3-1/2" x 4-9/16" (8.9 cm. x 11.6 cm.) Reproduction by Rolf P. Petersen. Collection of Mr. and Mrs. Daniel Dietrich, II, Philadelphia.

19. Eakins. Beach at Squan. 2-1/8" x 4-3/16" (5.3 cm. x 10.2 cm.) Reproduction by Rolf P. Petersen. Collection of Gordon Hendricks, New York.

20. Photographer unknown. Thomas Eakins as a boy. 4-9/16" x 4-1/16" (11.6 cm. x 8.7 cm.) Reproduction by William Pons. Collection of The Metropolitan Museum of Art, David Hunter McAlpin Fund, 1943.

21. Photographer unknown. Thomas Eakins. 4" x 4-1/16" (10.2 cm. x 9.1 cm.) Reproduction by Rolf P. Petersen. Collection of Mr. and Mrs. Daniel W. Dietrich, II, Philadelphia.

22. Photographer unknown. Thomas Eakins in a sailor suit. 4" x 3-9/16" (10.2 cm. x 9.1 cm.) Reproduction by Rolf P. Petersen. Collection of Mr. and Mrs. Daniel W. Dietrich, II, Philadelphia.

23. Photographer unknown. Thomas Eakins. 9-5/16" x 8-1/8" (23.7 cm. x 20.6 cm.) Reproduction by William Pons. Collection of The Metropolitan Museum of Art, Gift of Charles Bregler, 1961.

24. Photographer unknown. Thomas Eakins. 10" x 8-1/16" (25.4 cm. x 20.5 cm.) Reproduction by William Pons. Collection of The Metropolitan Museum of Art, Gift of Charles Bregler.

25. Photographer unknown. Thomas Eakins, engraving of Number 24. 9-1/2" x 12-1/2" (11.5 cm. x 16.5 cm.) Reproduction by Rolf P. Petersen. Collection of Gordon Hendricks, New York.

26. Photographer unknown. Thomas Eakins. 4-9/16" x 1-9/16" (11.6 cm. x 4 cm.) Reproduction by Rolf P. Petersen. Collection of Mr. and Mrs. Daniel W. Dietrich, II, Philadelphia.

27. Photographer unknown. Thomas Eakins. 6-7/16" x 5-3/16" (16.4 cm. x 13.2 cm.) Reproduction by Rolf P. Petersen. Collection of The Metropolitan Museum of Art, Gift of Charles Bregler.

Fig. 79. 28. Samuel Murray. Thomas Eakins. 4" x 5-1/8" (11.5 cm. x 16.5 cm.) Reproduction by A.J. Wyatt. Collection of the Philadelphia Museum of Art.

29. Photographer unknown. Thomas Eakins. Modern enlargement. Collection of Leonard Baskin, Northampton, Mass.

Fig. 81. 30. Photographer unknown. Thomas Eakins with Samuel Murray's sculpture of him. 4" x 5-1/4" (10.1 cm. x 13.3 cm.) Reproduction by Rolf P. Petersen. Collection of Gordon Hendricks, New York.

31. Photographer unknown. Thomas Eakins. 3-1/4" x 2-9/16" (8.2 cm. x 6.5 cm.) Reproduction by Rolf P. Petersen. Collection of Gordon Hendricks, New York.

31A. Photographer unknown. Thomas Eakins. 3-1/2" x 4-7/8" (8.9 cm. x 12.4 cm.) Reproduction by Rolf P. Petersen. Collection of Joseph Hirshhorn, New York.

32. Photographer unknown. Eakins in his fourth floor studio. 7" x 9-1/2" (17.8 cm. x 24.1 cm.) Reproduction by William Pons. Collection of The Metropolitan Museum of Art, Gift of Charles Bregler.

Fig. 82. 33. Samuel Murray? Thomas Eakins in the door of Mount Vernon Street house. c. 1915. 4-5/8" x 3-1/2" (11.7 cm. x 8.9 cm.) Reproduction by William Pons. Collection of The Metropolitan Museum of Art.

34. Photographer unknown. Thomas Eakins astride "Billy." 8" x 9-15/16" (20.3 cm. x 25.3 cm.) Reproduction by William Pons. Collection of The Metropolitan Museum of Art, Gift of Charles Bregler.

Fig. 80. 35. Photographer unknown. Thomas Eakins astride "Billy." Farm in Avondale. c. 1892. 10" x 8-1/8" (25.5 cm. x 20.6 cm.) Reproduction by A.J. Wyatt. Collection of the Philadelphia Museum of Art.

36. Photographer unknown. Thomas Eakins astride horse. Farm in Avondale. 4-1/2" x 3-1/16" (11.4 cm. x 7.8 cm.) Reproduction by Rolf P. Petersen. Collection of Mr. and Mrs. Daniel W. Dietrich, II, Philadelphia.

37. Photographer unknown. Thomas Eakins modeling horse statue for the Brooklyn Memorial Arch. Glass positive. 2-1/16" x 3-3/8" (5.2 cm. x 8.6 cm.) Reproduction by Rolf P. Petersen. Collection of Gordon Hendricks, New York.

38A. Photographer unknown. Benjamin Eakins. 5-1/2" x 3-9/16" (14 cm. x 9.1 cm.) Reproduction by Rolf P. Petersen. Collection of Gordon Hendricks, New York.

38B. Photographer unknown. Mrs. Benjamin Eakins. 6-1/2" x 4-15/16" (irreg.) (16.4 cm. x 12.6 cm.) Reproduction by Rolf P. Petersen. Collection of Gordon Hendricks, New York.

39. Photographer unknown. Frank Stephens. 5-1/4" x 4-3/4" (13.3 cm. x 12.1 cm.) Reproduction by Rolf P. Petersen. Collection of Donald Stephens, Arden, Delaware.

40. Photographer unknown. Thomas Eakins. 3-5/8" x 2-5/16" (9.2 cm. x 5.9 cm.) Reproduction by Rolf P. Petersen. Collection of Gordon Hendricks, New York.

41. Photographer unknown. Thomas Eakins. 3-9/16" x 2-7/16" (9 cm. x 6.2 cm.) Reproduction by Rolf P. Petersen. Collection of Gordon Hendricks, New York.

42. Photographer unknown. Caroline and Frances Eakins with two of Frances Eakins' children. Tintype. 3-11/16" x 2-1/2" (irreg.) (9.4 cm. x 6.4 cm.) Reproduction by Rolf P. Petersen. Collection of Gordon Hendricks, New York.

42A. Photographer unknown. Caroline Eakins, aged 15. *carte de visite.* 3-3/16" x 2-5/16" (8.1 cm. x 5.9 cm.) Reproduction by Rolf P. Petersen. Collection of Donald Stephens, Arden, Delaware.

43. Photographer unknown. Two girls under an umbrella. Tintype. 2-7/16" x 1-11/16" (6.2 cm. x 4.3 cm.) Reproduction by Rolf P. Petersen. Collection of Gordon Hendricks, New York.

44. Photographer unknown. Benjamin Eakins, *carte de visite.* 3-9/16" x 2-5/16" (9.1 cm. x 5.9 cm.) Reproduction by Rolf P. Petersen. Collection of Gordon Hendricks, New York.

45. Photographer unknown. Mrs. Benjamin Eakins, *carte de visite.* 3-5/8" x 2-5/16" (irreg.) (8.4 cm. x 5.9 cm.) Reproduction by Rolf P. Petersen. Collection of Gordon Hendricks, New York.

45A. Eakins. Margaret Eakins. Glass positive. 3-5/16" x 2-3/16" (8.4 cm. x 5.6 cm.) Reproduction by Rolf P. Petersen. Collection of Gordon Hendricks, New York.

46. Benjamin Eakins. Sample of Benjamin Eakins' handwriting. February 30, 1891. 3-15/16" x 8-9/16" (10 cm. x 21.8 cm.) Reproduction by Rolf P. Petersen. Collection of Gordon Hendricks, New York.

47. Benjamin Eakins. Sample of Benjamin Eakins' handwriting. November 2, 1885. 4" x 8-1/2" (10.2 cm. x 21.6 cm.) Reproduction by Rolf P. Petersen. Collection of Gordon Hendricks, New York.

48. Benjamin Eakins. Sample of Benjamin Eakins' handwriting. December 5, 1860. 4-7/16" x 8-1/4" (11.3 cm. x 21 cm.) Reproduction by Rolf P. Petersen. Collection of Gordon Hendricks, New York.

Fig. 51. 49. Eakins. Samuel Murray with his bust of Franklin Schenck. 1330 Chestnut Street studio. c. 1890. 3-15/16" x 4-15/16" (10 cm. x 12.5 cm.) Reproduction by A. J. Wyatt. Collection of the Philadelphia Museum of Art.

Fig. 50. 50. Eakins. Samuel Murray at work on his bust of Frank St. John. 3-9/16" x 4-1/2" (9.1 cm. x 11.5 cm.) Reproduction by Rolf P. Petersen. Collection of Mr. and Mrs. Daniel W. Dietrich, II, Philadelphia.

Fig. 65. 51. Eakins. Eakins' pupils at *The Swimming Hole* site. 1883? 5-15/16" x 7-3/4" (10 cm. x 19.7 cm.) Reproduction by Rolf P. Petersen. Collection of Joseph Hirshhorn, New York.

Fig. 61. 52. Eakins. Photograph from which the water-color *Drawing the Seine* was taken. Timber Creek estuary. 1882. 3-7/16" x 4-5/16" (8.8 cm. x 10.9 cm.) Reproduction by Rolf P. Petersen. Collection of Gordon Hendricks, New York.

Fig. 59. 53. Eakins. Shad fishing. Delaware River south of Gloucester, New Jersey. c. 1882. 3" x 4" (irreg.) (7.6 cm. x 10.2 cm.) Reproduction by Rolf P. Petersen. Collection of Gordon Hendricks, New York.

Fig. 58. 54. Eakins. *Hauling the Seine*, 1882. Oil on canvas. 12-1/2" x 18." Photograph courtesy of Cincinnati Art Museum. Collection of Cincinnati Art Museum.

Fig. 60. 55. Eakins. *Drawing the Seine*, 1882. Watercolor. 8" x 11." Photograph courtesy of the John G. Johnson Collection, Philadelphia. Collection of the John G. Johnson Collection, Philadelphia.

Fig. 35. 56. Eakins. Mr. and Mrs. William H. Macdowell on porch of their Race Street house. 4-1/2" x 6-3/8" (11.5 cm. x 16.2 cm.) Reproduction by Rolf P. Petersen. Collection of Walter Macdowell, Roanoke, Va.

57. Eakins. Mary (Dollie) Macdowell. 13-15/16" x 8-13/16" (35.4 cm. x 22.4 cm.) Reproduction by William Pons. Collection of The Metropolitan Museum of Art, David Hunter McAlpin Fund, 1943.

Fig. 43. 58. Eakins. Amelia C. Van Buren. c. 1891. 3-3/8" x 5-5/16" (8.6 cm. x 13.5 cm.) Reproduction by A.J. Wyatt. Collection of the Philadelphia Museum of Art.

Fig. 44. 59. Eakins. Amelia Van Buren. c. 1891. 5-15/16" x 3-7/8" (15.1 cm. x 9.9 cm.) Reproduction by Rolf P. Petersen. Collection of Mr. and Mrs. Daniel W. Dietrich, II, Philadelphia.

Fig. 15. 60. Eakins. Two of the artist's young relatives at the farm in Avondale. 2-11/16" x 4-1/4" (irreg.) (6.8 cm. x 10.5 cm.) Reproduction by Rolf P. Petersen. Collection of Gordon Hendricks, New York.

Fig. 12. 61. Eakins. Susan Macdowell and the Crowell children on the farm in Avondale. 3-7/16" x 4-6/16" (8.8 cm. x 11.1 cm.) Reproduction by Rolf P. Petersen. Collection of Gordon Hendricks, New York.

Fig. 19. 62. Eakins. The artist's niece, Katie Crowell, at the farm in Avondale. 2-3/16" x 2-1/8" (5.6 cm. x 5.4 cm.) Reproduction by Rolf P. Petersen. Collection of Gordon Hendricks, New York.

Fig. 16. 63. Eakins. Ben Crowell? 5-1/2" x 3-5/8" (14 cm. x 9.2 cm.) Reproduction by Rolf P. Petersen. Collection of Gordon Hendricks, New York.

Fig. 14. 65. Eakins. Two of the artist's nephews at the farm in Avondale. 3-1/2" x 4-3/8" (8.9 cm. x 10.7 cm.) Reproduction by Rolf P. Petersen. Collection of Gordon Hendricks, New York.

Fig. 13. 66. Eakins. Two of the artist's nephews at the farm in Avondale. 8-5/16" x 9-9/16" (21.1 cm. x 24.3 cm.) Reproduction by Rolf P. Petersen. Collection of Gordon Hendricks, New York.

Fig. 23. 67. Eakins. Tom Crowell. 3-3/4" x 2-5/16" (9.5 cm. x 5.9 cm.) Reproduction by Rolf P. Petersen. Collection of Gordon Hendricks, New York.

Fig. 9. 68. Eakins. Margaret Eakins. Mount Vernon Street. 4" x 3" (10.2 cm. x 7.6 cm.) Reproduction by Rolf P. Petersen. Collection of Gordon Hendricks, New York.

Fig. 10. 69. Eakins. Margaret Eakins in Eakins' Mount Vernon Street studio. 3-3/8" x 4-3/8" (8.6 cm. x 11.2 cm.) Reproduction by Rolf P. Petersen. Collection of Gordon Hendricks, New York.

Fig. 1. 70. Photographer unknown. Eakins' camera, lenses, plate holders, carrying case and palette. c. 1880+ Modern enlargement. Reproduction by Rolf P. Petersen. Collection of Gordon Hendricks, New York.

Fig. 57. 71. Eakins. Motion photograph of unidentified model. University of Pennsylvania. 1885. c. 4" x 5" (10.2 cm. x 12.7 cm.) Reproduction by the Franklin Institute. Collection of the Franklin Institute, Philadelphia.

Fig. 38. 73. Eakins. Women's modeling class at the Academy. Blanche Hurlbut seated on the floor at left. c. 1885. 6-13/16" x 8-7/16" (17.3 cm. x 21.5 cm.) Reproduction by William Pons. Collection of The Metropolitan Museum of Art, Gift of Charles Bregler.

Fig. 77. 74. Photographer unknown. Burlesque of *The Gross Clinic* with Eakins' Philadelphia Sketch Club with, possibly, Eakins at lower left. c. 1875. 4" x 5-1/16" (10.2 cm. x 12.9 cm.) Reproduction by A.J. Wyatt. Collection of the Philadelphia Museum of Art.

Fig. 36. 75. Eakins. William H. Macdowell. Mount Vernon Street yard. 7-3/8" x 4-5/8" (18.8 cm. x 11.8 cm.) Reproduction by Rolf P. Petersen. Collection of Gordon Hendricks, New York.

Fig. 33. 76. Eakins. William H. Macdowell. Race Street porch? 3-7/8" x 3-1/16" (9.9 cm. x 7.3 cm.) Reproduction by Rolf P. Petersen. Collection of Mr. and Mrs. Daniel W. Dietrich, II, Philadelphia.

Fig. 37. 77. Eakins. Mrs. William H. Macdowell. 9-15/16" x 8" (25.3 cm. x 20.3 cm.) Reproduction by William Pons. Collection of The Metropolitan Museum of Art, Gift of Charles Bregler.

Fig. 31. 78. Eakins. William H. Macdowell. Mount Vernon Street yard. 3-1/16" x 2-1/2" (irreg.) (7.8 cm. x 6.4 cm.) Reproduction by Rolf P. Petersen. Collection of Gordon Hendricks, New York.

Fig. 32. 80. Eakins. William H. Macdowell. Detail of Number 78; Fig. 31. 7-11/16" x 5-11/16" (19.5 cm. x 14.5 cm.) Reproduction by William Pons. Collection of The Metropolitan Museum of Art, David Hunter McAlpin Fund, 1943.

Fig. 66. 81. Eakins. *Arcadia*, 1883. Bas-relief. 21-1/2" x 25." Photograph courtesy of the Joseph Hirshhorn Collection, New York. Collection of Joseph Hirshhorn, New York.

Fig. 78. 82. J. Laurie Wallace? Thomas Eakins, 1883? 9" x 6-1/2" (22.9 cm. x 16.5 cm.) Reproduction by William Pons. Collection of The Metropolitan Museum of Art, David Hunter McAlpin Fund, 1943.

Fig. 67. 83. Eakins. Model J. Laurie Wallace posing with pan pipes in a landscape. c. 1883. 3-1/4" x 4-1/2" (8.2 cm. x 11.4 cm.) Reproduction by A.J. Wyatt. Collection of the Philadelphia Museum of Art.

Fig. 8.   84.   Eakins. W.H. Macdowell, Margaret Eakins
                  and two boys at Clinch Mountain. c. 1881.
                  10-7/8" x 7-7/8" (27.7 cm. x 20 cm.)
                  Reproduction by William Pons. Collection
                  of The Metropolitan Museum of Art, Gift
                  of Charles Bregler, 1941.

Fig. 11.   85.   Eakins. Margaret Eakins and Elizabeth
                  Macdowell at the farm in Avondale. 3-1/2" x
                  4-3/8" (8.9 cm. x 11.1 cm.) Reproduction
                  by Rolf P. Petersen. Collection of
                  Gordon Hendricks, New York.

Fig. 3.   86.   Eakins. Margaret Eakins and "Harry."
                  Mount Vernon Street yard. 4-5/8" x 5-1/4"
                  (11.8 cm. x 13.4 cm.) Reproduction by Rolf
                  P. Petersen. Collection of Gordon Hendricks,
                  New York.

Fig. 22.   87.   Eakins. Caroline Eakins. 4-9/16" x 3-1/4"
                  (11.6 cm. x 8.3 cm.) Reproduction by Rolf P.
                  Petersen. Collection of Gordon Hendricks,
                  New York.

Fig. 21.   88.   Eakins. Caroline Eakins with a dog. 4-1/2"
                  x 3-7/16" (11.4 cm. x 8.8 cm.) Reproduction
                  by Rolf P. Petersen. Collection of Gordon
                  Hendricks, New York.

Fig. 20.   89.   Eakins. Frances Eakins Crowell and, from
                  the left, on the first step, Artie, Ben,
                  and Will; Margaret or Ella (Eleanor) on
                  the second step; W.J. Crowell and Katie on
                  the third step; Jim, Margaret or Ella and Tom
                  on the fourth step. At the farm in Avondale.
                  9-7/8" x 13-9/16" (25.1 cm. x 34.5 cm.)
                  Reproduction by William Pons. Collection of
                  The Metropolitan Museum of Art, Gift of
                  Charles Bregler, 1944.

Fig. 17.   90.   Eakins. Frances Eakins Crowell and, from
                  the left, Katie, James W. and Frances
                  Crowell. Farm in Avondale. 7-3/4" x 7-7/8"
                  (19.7 cm. x 20 cm.) Reproduction by Rolf P.
                  Petersen. Collection of Gordon Hendricks,
                  New York.

Fig. 18.   91.   Eakins. Frances Eakins Crowell and three
                  of her children. 6-5/8" x 6-1/4" (16.9 cm.
                  x 15.9 cm.) Reproduction by Rolf P. Petersen.
                  Collection of Gordon Hendricks, New York.

           92A.   Eakins. Susan Macdowell. 5-9/16" x 2-1/2"
                  (14.2 cm. x 6.4 cm.) Reproduction by Rolf
                  P. Petersen. Collection of Joseph Hirshhorn,
                  New York.

Fig. 71.   92B.   Eakins. Reclining boy, playing pipes. Ben
                  Crowell? 5" x 8-13/16" (12.7 cm. x 22.4
                  cm.) Reproduction by Rolf P. Petersen.
                  Collection of Joseph Hirshhorn, New York.

           93A.   Eakins. Standing flute player. J. Laurie
                  Wallace. 3-5/16" x 3-7/16" (8.4 cm. x
                  8.7 cm.) Reproduction by O.E. Nelson.
                  Collection of Joseph Hirshhorn, New York.

Fig. 63.   93B.   Eakins. Wrestlers, top wrestler possibly
                  Joseph McCann. 1889? 3-1/2" x 5-3/4"
                  (8.9 cm. x 14.6 cm.) Reproduction by Rolf
                  P. Petersen. Collection of Joseph Hirshhorn,
                  New York.

Fig. 69.   94.   Eakins. *Arcadia*, 1883. Oil on canvas.
                  38-3/4" x 45-1/2". Photograph courtesy of
                  The Metropolitan Museum of Art. Collection
                  of The Metropolitan Museum of Art, bequest
                  of Miss Adelaide Milton de Groot (1876-1967),
                  1967.

Fig. 62.   95.   Eakins. *The Wrestlers*, 1899. Oil on canvas.
                  48" x 60". Photograph courtesy of the
                  Frick Art Reference Library. Collection
                  of the National Academy of Design, New York.

Fig. 41.   96.   Eakins. Sailboats. Delaware River? 3-1/8" x
                  4-7/8" (7.9 cm. x 12.4 cm.) Reproduction
                  by A. J. Wyatt. Collection of the
                  Philadelphia Museum of Art.

Fig. 24.   97.   Eakins. Crowell farm hand? 3-13/16" x
                  2-11/16" (9.7 cm. x 6.8 cm.) Reproduction
                  by Rolf P. Petersen. Collection of Gordon
                  Hendricks, New York.

Fig. 25.   98.   Eakins. "Old Margaret." Eakins'(?) servant.
                  3-7/16" x 2-7/8" (8.8 cm. x 7.4 cm.)
                  Reproduction by Rolf P. Petersen.
                  Collection of Gordon Hendricks, New York.

Fig. 6.   99.   Eakins. Benjamin Eakins in Mount Vernon
                  Street yard. 2-3/4" x 3-1/8" (7 cm. x
                  7.9 cm.) Reproduction by Rolf P. Petersen.
                  Collection of Mr. and Mrs. Daniel W.
                  Dietrich, II, Philadelphia.

Fig. 7.   100.   Eakins. Benjamin Eakins in Mount Vernon
                  Street yard. 4" x 3-1/4" (10.2 cm. x 8.3
                  cm.) Reproduction by Rolf P. Petersen.
                  Collection of Mr. and Mrs. Daniel W.
                  Dietrich, II, Philadelphia.

           101.   Photographer unknown. Thomas Eakins,
                  Samuel Murray and O'Donovan at Eakins'
                  1330 Chestnut Street studio. 4-11/16" x
                  6-1/2" (11.9 cm. x 16.5 cm.) Reproduction
                  by Rolf P. Petersen. Collection of
                  Joseph Hirshhorn, New York.

Fig. 5.   102.   Eakins. Cat. 4-11/16" x 2-5/8" (11.9 cm. x
                  6.7 cm.) Reproduction by Rolf P. Petersen.
                  Collection of Joseph Hirshhorn, New York.

Fig. 53.   103.   Eakins. Mrs. Anna Kershaw. 8-7/16" x
                  6-3/16" (21.4 cm. x 5.7 cm.) Reproduction
                  by Rolf P. Petersen. Collection of Joseph
                  Hirshhorn, New York.

Fig. 54.   104.   Eakins? Jennie-Dean Kershaw (later Mrs.
                  Samuel Murray). 1330 Chestnut Street
                  studio? 5" x 4" (12.7 cm. x 10.2 cm.)
                  Reproduction by Rolf P. Petersen.
                  Collection of Joseph Hirshhorn, New York.

Fig. 75. 105. Eakins. *Frank Hamilton Cushing*, 1895. Oil on canvas. 90" x 60." Photograph courtesy of the Thomas Cilcrease Institute of American History and Art, Tulsa, Oklahoma. Collection of the Thomas Gilcrease Institute of American History and Art, Tulsa, Oklahoma.

Fig. 76. 106. Eakins. Frank Hamilton Cushing. 1895. 5-5/8" x 4-3/4" (14.3 cm. x 12.1 cm.) Reproduction by Rolf P. Petersen. Collection of Joseph Hirshhorn, New York.

Fig. 56. 107. Eakins. *Mrs. Samuel Murray*, c. 1897. Oil on canvas. 40" x 30." Photograph courtesy of F.M. Hall Collection, University of Nebraska, Lincoln, Nebraska. Collection of F.M. Hall, University of Nebraska, Lincoln, Nebraska.

Fig. 55. 108. Eakins. *Mrs. Anna Kershaw*, 1903. Oil on canvas. 24" x 20." Photograph courtesy of Brenwasser Studio, New York.

Fig. 52. 109. Eakins. George W. Holmes, blind painter and teacher. 10-7/16" x 8-1/16" (26.5 cm. x 20.5 cm.) Reproduction by William Pons. Collection of The Metropolitan Museum of Art, David Hunter McAlpin Fund, 1943.

Fig. 45. 110. Eakins. Walt Whitman. First floor sitting room in Whitman's Camden house. 3-3/4" x 4" (9.5 cm. x 10.2 cm.) Reproduction by Rolf P. Petersen. Collection of Yale University, New Haven, Connecticut.

Fig. 47. 111. Eakins. Walt Whitman. Second floor bedroom in Whitman's Camden house. 1891. 7" x 4-7/8" (17.8 cm. x 12.4 cm.) Reproduction by A.J. Wyatt. Collection of the Philadelphia Museum of Art.

Fig. 46. 112. Eakins. Walt Whitman. Second floor bedroom in Whitman's Camden house. 3-3/4" x 4-3/4" (9.5 cm. x 12 cm.) Reproduction by A.J. Wyatt. Collection of the Philadelphia Museum of Art.

113. Eakins. *Walt Whitman*, 1887. Oil on canvas. 30" x 24". Photograph courtesy of the Pennsylvania Academy of the Fine Arts. Collection of the Pennsylvania Academy of the Fine Arts.

114. Eakins. Walt Whitman. Second floor bedroom in Whitman's Camden house. 3-3/4" x 5" (9.5 cm. x 12.7 cm.) Reproduction by A.J. Wyatt. Collection of the Philadelphia Museum of Art.

Fig. 48. 115. Eakins. *Walt Whitman*, c. 1887. Oil on wood, sketch for Number 113. 5-1/4" x 5-1/4". Photograph courtesy of the Boston Museum of Fine Arts. Collection of the Boston Museum of Fine Arts, Helen and Alice Colburn Fund.

117. Eakins. Amelia Van Buren. 8-1/4" x 6-11/16" (18.3 cm. x 17 cm.) Reproduction by William Pons. Collection of Metropolitan Museum of Art, David Hunter McAlpin Fund, 1943.

118. Eakins. "History of a Jump" with Eadweard Muybridge's notes. 3-1/2" x 5" (8.9 cm. x 12.7 cm.) Reproduction by Rolf P. Petersen. Collection of Gordon Hendricks, New York.

119. Eakins. J. Laurie Wallace, in a Marey wheel photograph. 10-1/8" x 10" (25.7 cm. x 25.5 cm.) Reproduction by the Franklin Institute. Collection of the Franklin Institute, Philadelphia.

120. Eakins. Samuel Murray astride a horse. 3-3/16" x 3-7/16" (8.1 cm. x 8.8 cm.) Reproduction by O.E. Nelson. Collection of Joseph Hirshhorn, New York.

121. Eakins. Geese, study for *Mending the Net*, Number 123. 3-15/16" x 7-1/4" (10 cm. x 18.4 cm.) Reproduction by Rolf P. Petersen. Collection of Joseph Hirshhorn, New York.

123. Eakins. *Mending the Net*, 1881. Oil on canvas. 32" x 45." Photograph courtesy of the Philadelphia Museum of Art. Collection of the Philadelphia Museum of Art.

124. Eakins. Margaret Eakins, Artie Crowell, Susan Macdowell. 3-1/2" x 4-1/4" (8.9 cm. x 10.8 cm.) Reproduction by Rolf P. Petersen. Collection of Gordon Hendricks, New York.

125. Eakins. Tom Crowell, Frances Eakins Crowell, Artie Crowell, Susan Macdowell and "Harry." 3-7/16" x 4-9/16" (irreg.) (8.8 cm. x 11.6 cm.) Reproduction by Rolf P. Petersen. Collection of Gordon Hendricks, New York.

126. Eakins. W.J. Crowell, Kathyrn Crowell and "Piero." 3-1/2" x 4-7/16" (8.9 cm. x 11.3 cm.) Reproduction by Rolf P. Petersen. Collection of Gordon Hendricks, New York.

126A. Eakins. W.J. Crowell, Kathryn Crowell and "Piero." Cropped enlargement of Number 126. 5-1/2" x 6-1/4" (irreg.) (14 cm. x 15.9 cm.) Reproduction by Rolf P. Petersen. Collection of Gordon Hendricks, New York.

128. Eakins. Caroline Eakins. 4-1/2" x 3-1/4" (11.5 cm. x 8.2 cm.) Reproduction by Rolf P. Petersen. Collection of Gordon Hendricks, New York.

129. Eakins. Ella or Margaret Crowell. 3-7/8" x 3-1/8" (9.9 cm. x 8 cm.) Reproduction by Rolf P. Petersen. Collection of Gordon Hendricks, New York.

130. Eakins. Caroline Eakins with a dog. 4-3/8" x 3-1/4" (11.2 cm. x 8.2 cm.) Reproduction by Rolf P. Petersen. Collection of Gordon Hendricks, New York.

131. Eakins. Caroline Eakins. 4-15/16" x 3-5/16" (11 cm. x 8.4 cm.) Reproduction by Rolf P. Petersen. Collection of Gordon Hendricks, New York.

132. Eakins. Caroline Eakins Stephens and baby. 3-5/8" x 4-5/8" (8.4 cm. x 11 cm.) Reproduction by Rolf P. Petersen. Collection of Donald Stephens, Arden, Delaware.

133. Eakins. Caroline Eakins. 4-1/4" x 3-3/4" (10.8 cm. x 9.5 cm.) Reproduction by Rolf P. Petersen. Collection of Donald Stephens, Arden, Delaware.

134. Eakins. Margaret Eakins. Modern enlargement. Reproduction by William Pons. Collection of The Metropolitan Museum of Art.

135. Eakins. Margaret Eakins. 2-3/4" x 2-1/2" (7 cm. x 6.4 cm.) Reproduction by Rolf P. Petersen. Collection of Gordon Hendricks, New York.

136. Photographer unknown. Camera. 3-1/4" x 2-7/8" (8.3 cm. x 7.3 cm.) Reproduction by Rolf P. Petersen. Collection of Joseph Hirshhorn, New York.

137. Eakins. "Harry." 8" x 6" (20.3 cm. x 15.2 cm.) Reproduction by Rolf P. Petersen. Collection of Gordon Hendricks, New York.

138. Eakins. Margaret Eakins atop "Harry's" kennel. 2-1/16" x 3-1/2" (5.2 cm. x 8.9 cm.) Reproduction by Rolf P. Petersen. Collection of Gordon Hendricks, New York.

139. Eakins. Margaret Eakins atop "Harry's" kennel. 2-13/16" x 3-3/8" (5.6 cm. x 8.6 cm.) Reproduction by Rolf P. Petersen. Collection of Mr. and Mrs. Daniel Dietrich,II, Philadelphia.

140. Eakins. Margaret Eakins with "Harry" in her lap. 2-1/4" x 2" (5.7 cm. x 5.1 cm.) Reproduction by Rolf P. Petersen. Collection of Gordon Hendricks, New York.

141. Eakins. "Harry" with an Irish setter. Side yard at Mount Vernon Street. 3-3/8" x 4-1/4" (8.6 cm. x 10.8 cm.) Reproduction by Rolf P. Petersen. Collection of Gordon Hendricks, New York.

142. Eakins. Horse and dog. North Dakota? 8-1/16" x 9-15/16" (20.5 cm. x 25.2 cm.) Reproduction by William Pons. Collection of The Metropolitan Museum of Art, Gift of Charles Bregler.

143. Eakins. "Augustus." 2-9/16" x 2-1/8" (6.5 cm. x 5.4 cm.) Reproduction by Rolf P. Petersen. Collection of Gordon Hendricks, New York.

144. Eakins. Cats. 2-15/16" x 5-1/16" (7.5 cm. x 12.9 cm.) Reproduction by Rolf P. Petersen. Collection of Mr. and Mrs. Daniel W. Dietrich, II, Philadelphia.

145. Eakins. Cats. 3-5/8" x 5" (9.2 cm. x 12.7 cm.) Reproduction by A.J. Wyatt. Collection of the Philadelphia Museum of Art.

146. Photographer unknown. Eakins and "Billy." Modern enlargement. Reproduction by A.J. Wyatt. Collection of the Philadelphia Museum of Art.

147. Eakins. Moving horse. 3-3/4" x 4-7/8" (9.5 cm. x 12.4 cm.) Reproduction by William Pons. Collection of The Metropolitan Museum of Art, New York, Gift of Charles Bregler.

148. Eakins. Men wrestling, used for *The Wrestlers*, Number 95. Modern enlargement. Reproduction by A.J. Wyatt. Collection of the Philadelphia Museum of Art.

149. Eadweard Muybridge. "Gaits of a Horse." 3-1/4" x 4-1/4" (8.2 cm. x 10.8 cm.) Reproduction by the Franklin Institute. Collection of the Franklin Institute, Philadelphia.

150. Eadweard Muybridge. "Gaits of a Horse." 3-1/4" x 4-1/4" (8.2 cm. x 10.8 cm.) Reproduction by the Franklin Institute. Collection of the Franklin Institute, Philadelphia.

151. Photographer unknown. Thomas Eakins. Marey wheel photograph. 3-15/16" x 5" (10 cm. x 12.7 cm.) Reproduction by William Pons. Collection of The Metropolitan Museum of Art, Gift of Charles Bregler, 1941.

152. Eakins. "History of a Jump." Marey wheel photograph. 3-5/8" x 4-7/8" (9.2 cm x 12.4 cm.) Reproduction by the Franklin Institute. Collection of the Franklin Institute, Philadelphia.

153. Eakins. Pennsylvania Academy of the Fine Arts' antique drawing class, with Adam Emory Albright at the right in front. 2-1/2" x 3-3/8" (6.4 cm. x 8.6 cm.) Reproduction by Rolf P. Petersen. Collection of Gordon Hendricks, New York.

154. Eakins. Pennsylvania Academy of the Fine Arts, mixed modeling class with a live horse. 4-5/8" x 7-3/4" (11.7 cm. x 19.7 cm.) Reproduction by Rolf P. Petersen. Collection of Gordon Hendricks, New York.

155. Eakins. Eakins' Academy students with skeletons of a horse and human. Modern enlargement. Reproduction by A.J. Wyatt. Collection of the Philadelphia Museum of Art.

156. Eakins. Academy instructor with pupils. 8" x 9-14/16" (20.3 cm. x 25.1 cm.) Reproduction by William Pons. Collection of The Metropolitan Museum of Art, Gift of Charles Bregler.

157. Eakins. Fairman Rogers astride "Josephine." 9-14/16" x 8" (25.1 cm. x 20.3 cm.) Reproduction by William Pons. Collection of The Metropolitan Museum of Art, Gift of Charles Bregler.

158. Eakins. George Reynolds pole vaulting. Marey wheel photograph. 3-5/8" x 4-3/4" (9.2 cm. x 12.1 cm.) Reproduction by A.J. Wyatt. Collection of the Philadelphia Museum of Art.

159. Eakins. Eakins' Academy pupils wrestling. 8-1/16" x 9-15/16" (20.5 cm. x 25.3 cm.) Reproduction by William Pons. Collection of The Metropolitan Museum of Art, Museum accession, 1961.

160. Eakins. Jesse Godley. Marey wheel photograph. 3-3/4" x 4-3/4" (9.5 cm. x 12.1 cm.) Reproduction by William Pons. Collection of The Metropolitan Museum of Art, Gift of Charles Bregler, 1941.

162. Eakins. Barnyard at the farm in Avondale. 2-7/8" x 4-5/8" (7.3 cm. x 11.8 cm.) Reproduction by Rolf P. Petersen. Collection of Gordon Hendricks, New York.

163. Eakins. Kathryn Cook with plaster torso. 3-3/16" x 2-5/16" (8.1 cm. x 5.9 cm.) Reproduction by Rolf P. Petersen. Collection of Mr. and Mrs. Daniel W. Dietrich, II, Philadelphia.

Fig. 40. 164. Eakins. Weda Cook with Academy plaster cast. 5-13/16" x 3-15/16" (5 cm. x 10 cm.) Reproduction by Rolf P. Petersen. Collection of Gordon Hendricks, New York.

165. Eakins. Weda Cook, profile. 5-3/4" x 3" (14.6 cm. x 7.6 cm.) Reproduction by Rolf P. Petersen. Collection of Gordon Hendricks, New York.

166. Eakins. Weda Cook, Kathryn Cook and Dorothy Cook. 3" x 2-7/8" (7.6 cm. x 7.3 cm.) Reproduction by Rolf P. Petersen. Collection of Gordon Hendricks, New York.

168. Photographer unknown. Horse. 3-15/16" x 5-5/16" (10 cm. x 13.5 cm.) Reproduction by Rolf P. Petersen. Collection of Joseph Hirshhorn, New York.

169. Eakins. Bust of an old man. 4" x 2-1/2" (10.2 cm. x 6.4 cm.) Reproduction by Rolf P. Petersen. Collection of Joseph Hirshhorn, New York.

170. Photographer unknown. Thomas Eakins. 10" x 8" (25.4 cm. x 20.3 cm.) Reproduction by Rolf P. Petersen. Collection of Joseph Hirshhorn, New York.

171. Photographer unknown. Thomas Eakins. 6-3/4" x 4-1/16" (17.2 cm. x 10.3 cm.) Reproduction by Rolf P. Petersen. Collection of Joseph Hirshhorn, New York.

172. Murray? Eakins working on Frank St. John's portrait. 3-11/16" x 4-6/16" (9.4 cm. x 11.1 cm.) Reproduction by Rolf P. Petersen. Collection of Joseph Hirshhorn, New York.

173. Murray. Mr. and Mrs. Thomas Eakins. 4-3/16" x 3-5/16" (10.2 cm. x 8.4 cm.) Reproduction by O.E. Nelson. Collection of Joseph Hirshhorn, New York.

174. Eakins. Murray in his shirt-sleeves. 3-5/16" x 3" (10 cm. x 7.6 cm.) Reproduction by Rolf P. Petersen. Collection of Joseph Hirshhorn, New York.

175. Photographer unknown. Mrs. Samuel Murray-to-be having her portrait painted. 4-7/16" x 3-14/16" (11.3 cm. x 9.9 cm.) Reproduction by Rolf P. Petersen. Collection of Joseph Hirshhorn, New York.

178. Photographer unknown. Eakins and Murray on the Cohannesy River. 4-5/16" x 6-1/16" (11 cm. x 15.4 cm.) Reproduction by Rolf P. Petersen. Collection of Joseph Hirshhorn, New York.

179. Eakins. Elizabeth Macdowell. Yard at Mount Vernon Street house. 3-9/16" x 4-3/8" (9.1 cm. x 11.1 cm.) Reproduction by Rolf P. Petersen. Collection of Joseph Hirshhorn New York.

Fig. 72. 180. Eakins. Eliza Cowperthwaite. 4-5/8" x 3-3/8" (11.8 cm. x 8.6 cm.) Reproduction by Rolf P. Petersen. Collection of Gordon Hendricks, New York.

180A. Eakins. Unknown woman. 4-1/8" x 3-3/16" (10.4 cm. x 8.1 cm.) Reproduction by Rolf P. Petersen. Collection of Gordon Hendricks, New York.

181. Eakins. Old woman. 2-5/8" x 3-3/8" (6.7 cm. x 8.1 cm.) Reproduction by Rolf P. Petersen. Collection of Gordon Hendricks, New York.

182. Eakins. Woman and child, study for *Arcadia*. 2" x 3-1/8" (5.1 cm. x 7.9 cm.) Reproduction by Rolf P. Petersen. Collection of Gordon Hendricks, New York.

183. Eakins. Adults and Eakins' nephews under a beech tree at the farm in Avondale (?). 8-11/16" x 6-3/4" (22.1 cm. x 17.2 cm.) Reproduction by Rolf P. Petersen. Collection of Gordon Hendricks, New York.

184. Eakins. Old woman, profile. 9-15/16" x 8-1/16" (25.3 cm. x 20.5 cm.) Reproduction by William Pons. Collection of The Metropolitan Museum of Art, Gift of Charles Bregler.

185. Eakins. Artie Crowell and an unidentified girl. 3-5/8" x 2-3/4" (irreg.) (9.2 cm. x 7 cm.) Reproduction by Rolf P. Petersen. Collection of Gordon Hendricks, New York.

186. Eakins. Artie Crowell. 3-3/8" x 4-1/2" (irreg.) (8.6 cm. x 11.4 cm.) Reproduction by Rolf P. Petersen. Collection of Gordon Hendricks, New York.

187. **Eakins.** Cowboy in regalia, North Dakota. 9-15/16" x 8-1/16" (25.3 cm. x 20.5 cm.) Reproduction by William Pons. Collection of The Metropolitan Museum of Art, Gift of Charles Bregler, 1961.

188. Eakins. Woman on pony, North Dakota. 8-1/16" x 9-15/16" (20.5 cm. x 25.3 cm.) Reproduction by William Pons. Collection of The Metropolitan Museum of Art, Gift of Charles Bregler.

189. Eakins. J. Laurie Wallace. 9" x 6-7/8" (22.9 cm. x 17.5 cm.) Reproduction by William Pons. Collection of The Metropolitan Museum of Art, David Hunter McAlpin Fund, 1943.

190. Photographer unknown. Eakins and J. Laurie Wallace. 10-3/8" x 8-1/16" (26.3 cm. x 20.5 cm.) Reproduction by William Pons. Collection of The Metropolitan Museum of Art, David Hunter McAlpin Fund, 1943.

Fig. 68. 191. Eakins. Girls in Greek costume. 14" x 10-1/16" (35.6 cm. x 25.5 cm.) Reproduction by William Pons. Collection of The Metropolitan Museum of Art, David Hunter McAlpin Fund, 1943.

192. Eakins. Girls in Greek costume, dancing. 5-1/2" x 6-15/16" (14 cm. x 17.7 cm.) Reproduction by Rolf P. Petersen. Collection of Joseph Hirshhorn, New York.

Fig. 34. 193. Eakins. William H. Macdowell. 5-11/16" x 6-9/16" (14.5 cm. x 16.7 cm.) Reproduction by William Pons. Collection of The Metropolitan Museum of Art, David Hunter McAlpin Fund, 1943.

194. Eakins. *The Oboe Player*, 1903. Oil on canvas. 36" x 24." Photograph courtesy of the Philadelphia Museum of Art. Collection of the Philadelphia Museum of Art.

195. Eakins. Study for *The Oboe Player*, Number 194. One col. width Reproduction by Rolf P. Petersen. Collection of Gordon Hendricks, New York.

196. Eakins. Trees on Frances Crowell's farm in Avondale. 3-9/16" x 4-7/16" (irreg.) (9.1 cm. x 11.3 cm.) Reproduction by Rolf P. Petersen. Collection of Gordon Hendricks, New York.

197. Eakins. *An Arcadian*, 1883. Oil on canvas. 14" x 18." Photograph courtesy of Lloyd Goodrich. Collection of Lloyd Goodrich, New York

198. Eakins. Eakins' pupils at *The Swimming Hole* site. 3-1/8" x 3-3/4" (7.9 cm. x 9.5 cm.) Reproduction by Rolf P. Petersen. Collection of Joseph Hirshhorn, New York.

200. Eakins. Eakins' Academy pupils. Modern enlargement. Reproduction by A.J. Wyatt. Collection of the Philadelphia Museum of Art.

201. Eakins. Seated man. 5" x 4" (12.7 cm. x 10.2 cm.) Reproduction by A.J. Wyatt. Collection of the Philadelphia Museum of Art.

202. Eakins. Seated Man. 9-1/4" x 8-5/8" (23.5 cm. x 21.9 cm.) Reproduction by William Pons. Collection of The Metropolitan Museum of Art, David Hunter McAlpin Fund, 1943.

203. Eakins. Schenck in Eakins' 1330 Chestnut Street studio with a tug-of-war apparatus. 9-15/16" x 8" (25.2 cm. x 20.3 cm.) Reproduction by William Pons. Collection of The Metropolitan Museum of Art, Gift of Charles Bregler, 1961.

204. Eakins. Charles Brinton Cox drawing a male model. 6-13/16" x 5-7/16" (17.3 cm. x 13.9 cm.) Reproduction by William Pons. Collection of The Metropolitan Museum of Art, David Hunter McAlpin Fund, 1943.

205. Eakins. Female model. 2-13/16" x 5-1/4" (7.2 cm. x 13.3 cm.) Reproduction by William Pons. Collection of The Metropolitan Museum of Art, David Hunter McAlpin Fund, 1943.

206. Eakins. William G. Macdowell. 4-1/16" x 3-1/16" (10.3 cm. x 7.8 cm.) Reproduction By Rolf P. Petersen. Collection of Walter Macdowell, Roanoke, Va.

207. Eakins. William G. Macdowell, vignette of Number 206. 4-1/8" x 3-1/16" (10.5 cm. x 7.8 cm.) Reproduction by Rolf P. Petersen. Collection of Walter Macdowell, Roanoke, Va.

208. Photographer unknown. Eakins and G.W. Holmes. 10-1/4" x 12" (irreg.) (26.1 cm. x 30.5 cm.) Reproduction by the Franklin Institute. Collection of the Franklin Institute, Philadelphia.

Fig. 49. 209. Eakins. *Frank St. John*, 1900. Oil on canvas. 24-1/2" x 20-1/2." Photograph courtesy of Kennedy Galleries. Collection of Kennedy Galleries, New York.

Fig. 42. 210. Eakins. *Amelia Van Buren*, 1891. Oil on canvas. 45" x 32." Photograph courtesy of the Phillips Collection. Collection of the Phillips Collection, Washington, D.C.

211. Eakins. Mrs. Samuel Murray. 4-1/8" x 3-9/16" (10.5 cm. x 9 cm.) Reproduction by A.J. Wyatt. Collection of the Philadelphia Museum of Art.

Fig. 39. 213. Eakins. *The Concert Singer*, 1892. Oil on canvas. 75" x 54." Photograph courtesy of the Philadelphia Museum of Art. Collection of the Philadelphia Museum of Art.

Fig. 64. 215. Eakins. *The Swimming Hole*, 1883. Oil on canvas. 27" x 36." Photograph courtesy of the Fort Worth Art Center. Collection of the Fort Worth Art Center, Fort Worth, Texas.

Index

Designed by Eugene Feldman and printed at
The Falcon Press, Philadelphia